editorial coordination
Giovanna Crespi
graphic design
Tassinari/Vetta
page layout
Claudia Brambilla
editorial coordination
Virginia Ponciroli
editing
Gail Swerling
translation
Christopher Evans
picture research
Rosa Chiesa
Stefania Colonna-Preti
cover graphics
Tassinari/Vetta
technical coordination
Andrea Panozzo
quality control
Giancarlo Berti

Distributed by Phaidon Press
ISBN 978-1-9043-1356-4

www.phaidon.com

www.electaweb.com

First published in English in 2007

Printed in China

To Diego and Augusto

LATIN AMERICAN HOUSES

Electaarchitecture

mercedes daguerre

andrade & morettin
alejandro aravena
javier artadi
felipe assadi
barclay & crousse
clusellas & colle
ga grupo arquitectura / daniel alvarex
alberto kalach
mathias klotz
marcio kogan
leopoldo laguinge
lbc arquitectos / alfonso lópez baz and javier calleja
lcm / fernando romero
paulo mendes da rocha
mmbb arquitetos / angelo bucci
procter & rihl
smiljan radic
michel rojkind
cristián undurraga

el juego del revés
the backwards game

mercedes daguerre

Selecting a few houses to represent the contemporary architectural scene in Latin America is obviously a highly arbitrary undertaking. The whole thing is rendered even more tentative by the fact that the geographical and cultural notion of "Latin America" is in itself problematic. A category that embraces a territory stretching from the Rio Grande to the Tierra del Fuego, full of contrasts and contradictions, where Christianity, the Spanish tongue and architecture have been the three great colonial legacies left by Spain. Three "languages" that are supposed to have structured a hypothetical "unity" over the course of the last five centuries.[1] As recent studies have demonstrated, however, the certainty about the effects that these centripetal forces still exercise today (with of course the exceptions of Brazil, conquered by the Portuguese, and the Caribbean countries colonized by the British and Dutch) on Latin American architectural culture is undermined by the wide variety of independent expressions, as well as by the instability of processes of democratization. And yet it is evident that, after the disruption caused by the subcontinent's entry into the world market at the end of the nineteenth century, new tendencies of cohesion have emerged over the course of the twentieth century and are still in operation at the beginning of the new millennium. These have affected different spheres, from politics to literature and art, from economics to social protest and the questions of indigenous rights and the environment.[2] A complexity that must be taken into account on the concrete plane of architecture, by recognizing the multiplicity of factors at work in this contradictory and fertile common culture.

Without any pretension to being exhaustive and with no ambition to explain the full range and variety of situations out of which the works illustrated here have sprung, we nevertheless intend to present a sufficiently significant sample of detached houses designed by architects active in Latin American countries: architects who have different backgrounds and levels of expressive maturity and come from different generations. We shall attempt to place them in a frame of reference that, however fragmentary, will permit the reader to approach these different realities from a more lucid and dispassionate perspective than the one to which the "official" critical historiography has accustomed us.[3]

Recognizing the extreme subjectivity of the approach adopted, and resisting any temptation to apply the term "Latin American" as a one-size-fits-all label, we think it opportune to point out that such a qualification might help to avoid the folkloristic effect to which leads, in the view of Jorge Liernur, "the analysis of a peripheral product carried out according to rules of play and evaluation generated and dominated by metropolitan cultures and thus inserted in a sort of gallery of peers that, by definition, are nothing of the kind."[4] Obliged, therefore, to reckon with processes of modernization that are continually oscillating between "civilization and barbarism," Latin American architects also have to cope with the rapid multiplication of the centers of reference resulting from globalization.[5]

However, the objective impossibility of a comparison *inter pares* with the architectural production of the industrialized countries should not prevent identification of the potentialities implicit in this research. It is true that the development of the market economy has led to a wider diffusion of models and relations—something that was already taking place, moreover, as part of the various processes of modernization—And an accentuated mobility of the operators themselves (often young architects, whose training has not been limited to the context of their own country's academic structures, but has found opportunities for growth and the exchange of ideas in experiences abroad, at prestigious universities or working with the most successful contemporary architects). Yet it is evident that their works reflect a whole set of "intercultural" problems that are anything but equivalent, where the profession, the practices of construction and the changes in the discipline express different traditions, as well as professional characteristics rooted in different institutional contexts.

Thus proposing a range of domestic architecture emerging from this geographical region, which illustrates trends, conflicts and questions of a disciplinary world that is to some extent unfamiliar to much of the European public, could turn out to be extremely useful in stimulating reflection and prompting contributions to the wider debate over the design of the detached house. It is also to be hoped that, notwithstanding the

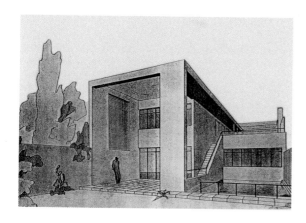

Wladimiro Acosta, house of the journalist Raúl de Polillo, São Paulo, Brazil, 1931.

Le Corbusier, Casa Curutchet, La Plata, Argentina, 1949.

limitations from which it starts out, this collection will offer some keys to the interpretation and understanding of the "architectures" of Latin America, arousing not just curiosity devoid of exoticism, but also a real interest in going beyond the habitual cursory examination of peripheral experiences to be found in specialist publications.

Even though the fact of focusing our attention on a theme intended for the middle and upper class offers a greater margin of possibility for architectural experimentation, the structural conditionings are certainly crucial when it comes to evaluating the "qualitative" production of the individual countries, taking account not only of the exceptional character of the cases illustrated, but also of the concrete conditions of the profession and the level of the disciplinary debate.[6] It is no surprise, therefore, that the results of the detailed investigation that preceded this selection, while totally provisional, have identified Chile, Brazil and Mexico as emergent centers on the overall architectural scene, along with promising areas, like Peru, or situations of extreme difficulty, as in Argentina and Uruguay. They have also brought to light some significant absences (it suffices to think of Venezuela and Colombia, to cite just two revealing examples).

Latin America: Living in the Modern

Drawing on familiar archetypes of the modern tradition, not always univocal and frequently superimposed on one another in the lineage of the same design, as well as always bearing clearly in mind the best-known works of the various local "modernisms" that filter and rework the sources, these detached houses have a very broad horizon of reference that requires considerable depth of understanding from the critic. From the designs of brick or courtyard houses produced by Mies van der Rohe in the twenties and thirties to those of Resor House (1937–38) or Farnsworth House (1945–50), from his American period; from the white houses of the *Les Cahiers de la Recherche*, culminating in the emblematic Ville Savoye (1929), to the vernacular Le Corbusier of La Celle Saint Cloud (1935) or the Maisons Jaoul at Neuilly-sur-Seine (1952); from Frank Lloyd Wright's simultaneous exploration of old and new technologies in the Usonian Houses to his confrontation with the dimensions of the desert (Taliesin West, Scottsdale, 1937–38); from the Californian residences created in the thirties by Richard Neutra and Rudolph Schindler, with their courtyards, porches and large expanses of glass, to the later Case Study Houses, influenced by Aalto in their use of natural materials or by the relationship with the site established by Adalberto Libera in his Casa Malaparte on Capri (1938–42).[7]

Apparent right from the start, however, is a contradictory aspect that fosters, even in our own day, a cultural stereotype in the European architectural debate. While, from the thirties onward, the most talented architects in Latin America looked to the different expressions of modernity, in search of a renewal and of the instruments they needed to overcome their own structural backwardness, it is paradoxical that it was the "primitivism" of these latitudes that proved of interest to many lines of avant-garde research that were looking at the time for alternative ways of promoting original and "authentic" values.[8] For many figures of modern Latin American architecture, in fact, the revival of local values was not at all in conflict with the language of modernity: Julio Vilamajó in Uruguay, Alberto Prebisch and Antonio Vilar in Argentina, Lúcio Costa in Brazil, Carlos Raúl Villanueva in Venezuela or Juan O'Gorman and Enrique del Moral in Mexico are all illuminating examples of this. And not coincidentally, as has been pointed out on several occasions, the building symbolic of the birth of the modern in Latin America, the Ministry of Education (1936–45) designed by Le Corbusier and his disciples in Rio de Janeiro, is regarded as such precisely for the way that it assimilates elements typical of the Brazilian architectural tradition.[9]

With an extremely varied heritage of historical buildings, from the pre-Columbian vestiges of Peru, Guatemala or Mexico to the colonial baroque of Brazil and Paraguay and the cultural hybridization of the society of the Southern Cone with its high levels of immigration (Argentina, Uruguay, Chile), the Latin American versions of modernism have found numerous stimuli and motifs of marked characterization in this frame of reference. The cultural obliteration carried out during the various phases of "conquest" (Spanish, Portuguese, British, French, Dutch and, lastly, North American) aroused a strong demand for identity in the various countries of Latin America that, as early as the end of nineteenth century, found parallels in European reflections on the construction of a "national art."[10] Since that time, this theme has conditioned the debate on the relationship between architecture and history, generating a pressing need to define a "distinctive style." As we have had an opportunity to explain elsewhere, over the course of the twentieth century these theorizations became part of the debate over an alternative to the International Style and merged, subsequently, into the research into "new regionalisms," which was to find a fruitful field of inquiry in the theme of the detached house.[11]

The relationship of the modern with tradition is therefore an intrinsic element of the debate over modernisms in these latitudes. As is well known, a significant contribution to this

debate has been made, from the outset, by a number of architects in exile and illustrious guests, whose later work would bear the mark of their Latin American experience. This has resulted in a sort of reverberation of influences that has, in some cases, turned into a genuine "play of mirrors."

The South—Buenos Aires, Montevideo, Asunción, São Paulo and Rio de Janeiro—was seen by Le Corbusier, in 1929, as an extremely alluring "new world" for the realization of *grands traveaux* and, not coincidentally, his 1949 design for Casa Curutchet at La Plata, a careful blend of the new and the pre-existing, would represent a small "inventory" of the general strategy adopted by the Swiss master for the masterplan of Buenos Aires.[12]

At the end of the thirties, revolutionary Mexico seems to have been the only place that still welcomed exponents of the more radical avant-garde. The frustrations of Hannes Meyer or the successful integration of Max Cetto and Mathias Goeritz—close to the expressionist current in the years of their training—into the Mexican context are paradigmatic examples of the ups and downs the modern has been through on American soil.[13] Meyer's stay in Mexico City highlights, moreover, many of the contradictions already present in his previous experience (in Germany, the Soviet Union and Switzerland). His theories on regionalism came at a crucial moment in the Mexican architectural debate, shaped by the profound changes introduced by the Cárdenas administration in the third decade of the century. However, his condemnation of "international architecture" and consequent extolling of an approach to design based on "regionalist" principles amounted to an implicit criticism of the local functionalist current represented by Juan O'Gorman, who had had a considerable influence on state building policies after the revolution and had produced a fine display of his talents in the house for Frida Kahlo and Diego Rivera (1931): technological syncretism, exploration of textures and use of bright colors were to become characteristics of Mexican modern architecture. However—as Gorelik has pointed out—Meyer's regionalism was more political than linguistic, rooted rationally in a daily engagement with reality and not an ideological expression of cultural "essences": "technique" rather than "art."[14]

This approach marks his distance from the regionalism proposed by Le Corbusier in 1930 with his Errázuriz Villa (designed for a site on the Chilean coast and contemporary with both the playful surrealism of the Beistegui Apartment and the materiality of Maison Mandrot in Toulon), which paradoxically became—with its stone base, white-plastered walls and logs used for the structure of the tiled roof—an out-and-out paradigm of "autochthonous" values for much of the Latin American architecture of the forties. But it also diverges from the interest in the new national styles of architecture promoted by the New York World's Fair of 1939, where the Brazilian pavilion of Lúcio Costa and Oscar Niemeyer would bring the "case" of Brazil into the international debate. The lightness of the structure, the plastic equilibrium and elegance of form, the sinuosity of the ramp and the colors of Burle Marx's tropical garden were elements of a vocabulary that, from that time on, would be identified with modern Brazilian architecture by the specialist press.

The Ukrainian Gregori Warchavchik was certainly one of the "pioneers" in the introduction of the modern into Brazil. Through his detached houses—including the one on Via Santa Cruz in the style of Loos (1928)—he proposed an integration of art and architecture and promoted a search for innovative structural solutions to overcome the difficulty of spreading the new architecture with a labor force not trained in the use of reinforced concrete and without a building market able to supply standardized components.[15] Later other architects explored the new language, developing an unexpected virtuosity: it suffices to recall the residential works of Alfonso Eduardo Reidy, Jorge Machado Moreira, Alvaro Vital Brazil, Marcelo and Milton Roberto, Oswaldo Bratke and Sérgio Bernardes, as well as the well-known Casa Guper (1951–53), built by Rino Levi in São Paulo: one of the most successful products of the systematic research the architect embarked on from the time of his arrival in Brazil, in 1928, in which he experimented with the insertion of the Mediterranean patio into the new urban context. However, it was Le Corbusier's visit to Rio de Janeiro, in 1936, that gave a real boost to Brazilian modernism.[16]

Writing the introduction to Henrique Mindlin's *Modern Architecture in Brazil* twenty years after this "founding" event, Sigfried Giedion summed up the impression of admiration and bewilderment that this caused on the international scene. In his eyes it was precisely the "irrationality" of the development of modern Brazilian architecture, which "was growing like a tropical plant," spreading rapidly to the rest of the territory, that constituted the real problem. Its precarious character was evident in the face of the rapid expansion of urban centers, real-estate speculation, the absence of planning schemes and the failure to industrialize construction. Giedion's difficulty lay, first of all, in the impossibility of understanding the "mode" by which the modern had been absorbed in a country clearly split between the underdevelopment of its socioeconomic conditions and the high level of its erudite architectural creations. In those dynamics—which implied adoption of the planning procedures of the European

Juan O'Gorman, Rivera-Kahlo house-studio, Mexico City, Mexico, 1931.

Vilanova Antigas, the architect's second house, São Paulo, Brazil, 1949.
Max Cetto, Casa Cetto, El Pedregal, Mexico City, Mexico, 1949.

avant-garde, adapting them to the local circumstances—the role of Le Corbusier had undoubtedly been important, but wholly insufficient to explain the phenomenon.[17] To the criticism of formalism leveled by Max Bill at Brazilian architecture, guilty of having violated modernist orthodoxy by lying bare its own contradictions, the protagonists of this "anomaly" responded with perspicacity.[18] Niemeyer himself—genuine creator of icons for the young nation—would defend his own creative autonomy through the expressive possibilities of reinforced concrete, which had no need of excessive precision in construction and permitted utilization of the surplus of unskilled labor.[19]

According to the more perceptive critics, the peculiarity of this modernism, its "anti-avant-gardism" (where the basic problem is not an excess of history, but on the contrary its absence), lay precisely in the type of equation that had been made between it and the construction of a "national identity." It was the theoretical ideas of Lúcio Costa that became dominant in the country's architectural production. Clearly formulated in his *casas sem dono* (1932–36), these would be perfected in compositional exercises that investigated the connection between the scheme centered on the court and linearity, in the ambiguous relationship between exterior and interior inherited from colonial constructions. Thus Casa Saavedra (1942), with its mixed structure and sloping roofs, Casa Hungria Machado (1942) or Casa Paes de Carvalho (1944) in Rio de Janeiro, reconciling patios and galleries, tile roofs and strip windows protected by movable blinds, accentuate the introspection and propose a new spatiality. An approach in which modern architecture is presented as a link with the "true spirit" of the Brazilian tradition and where identity is therefore not simply recovered from the past, but is a notion that is created by projecting it into the future. Turning on its head the "tradition of the new" theorized at the Bauhaus, Costa overcame the simple dichotomy between traditional and modern: so the canonical version of Brazilian modernism was to produce "artistic objects" that do not live solely in the present, but simultaneously generate a future and a tradition. In this sense, the Brazilian interpretation of Le Corbusier's link between technique and lyricism is made manifest, in its most elaborate formulations, in a dimension of expression in which the structure becomes predominant.[20] Out of all this came an extremely effective mechanism, which embraced the magnificent experiments of the forties within a new synthesis, in which classicizing compositions and clearly modern solutions were combined with simplicity, making use of local typologies and materials; solutions focused on the identification of new ways of constructing a national language.[21]

The strong demand for public works led to a spread of Brazilian modernism through the rest of the country, and this was given further impetus by the success of a second wave of European architects, lured to South America by the growing opportunities for work offered by a rapidly expanding economy (among them, Lina Bo Bardi, Daniele Calabi, Giancarlo Palanti and Bernard Rudofsky). The criticisms leveled at Brasilia—epitome of the modern capital, founded in 1957 as a demonstration of the capacity of the new language to take on the symbolic representation of the power of the State— would bring a cycle to a close.[22] Even though Brazilian architecture definitively lost its role as a protagonist of the international scene, this phase of metropolitan development saw an intensification of the construction of new typologies of buildings and residential districts in which, instead of applying the *Existenz-minimum*, an attempt was made to adapt the advantages of the detached house to the new housing programs, creating works of architecture of remarkable quality. To understand the extent to which the scale of housing was seen by the principal architects of the period as a privileged laboratory for experimentation with form, space and construction, it suffices to take a quick look at a few emblematic examples, point of arrival of earlier explorations but also reification of some of the different approaches that interacted in the Brazilian architectural debate of the period. The second house that Vilanova Artigas built for his own family in São Paulo in 1949 (concrete butterfly-wing roof conceived as an inversion of the pitched roof, bilateral symmetry, interconnection of the different rooms) is a clear expression of the critical radicalism that characterizes his proposals, in which the typology, the program and even the values of the bourgeois house are brought into question. In the Glass House (1949–51) designed by Lina Bo Bardi at Morumbi, the transparent box set on steel pilotis and perforated by a metal staircase and a tree that penetrates into the living room expresses the duality of the structural solution with respect to the wing of the bedrooms, anchored to the rock. It is the entrance route, oscillating between light and shade, that guides you toward the heart of the dwelling where, with cosmopolitan sophistication, domesticity is conceived as an ambivalent superimposition of artistic objects and allusions to the naïf. The Casa das Canoas (1952–53), built by Oscar Niemeyer in Rio di Janeiro and located on a platform created in the midst of thick vegetation, is conceived as a pavilion and a cave at one and the same time. The layout and the free-standing façade accentuate the sculptural character of the flat roof, whose sinuous edges soften the tension between nature and artifact in a refined symbiosis with the landscape. Residential designs that, by multiplying the references

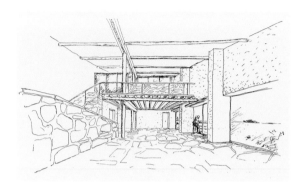

Le Corbusier, Casa Errázuriz, Chile, 1930.

Gregori Warchavchik, house on Rua Santa Cruz, São Paulo, Brazil, 1928.
Rino Levi, Casa Milton Guper, São Paulo, Brazil, 1951–53.

of "cultural cannibalism" theorized by the local literary and artistic avant-garde, enriched and encapsulate a figurative repertoire still found in contemporary Brazilian architecture.[23] Pragmatic and syncretic are the words that have been used to describe the reception that Chilean culture gave to the new ideas arriving from overseas, interpreted in exclusively formal terms within a strong classicist tradition. Some of Sergio Larraín's works exhibit an essentially stylistic adherence to modernism, oriented toward a cautious continuity rather than a radical break with the past. The arrival of Le Corbusier, to take part in the work of reconstruction after the heavy damage caused by the earthquake of 1939, sparked a controversy and divided professional circles in the capital. At that time several figures who had already adopted avant-garde positions emerged, going on to become protagonists of the architectural debate in the following decades, when modern design would be flanked by a precise "poetics of adaptation." Emilio Duhart's house at Las Condes (1946–49) or Casa Santos at Papudo (1958), designed by Carlos Bresciani, Héctor Valdés, Fernando Castillo and Carlos Huidobro, clearly express the sensitivity with which the local modernism investigated— through formal abstraction and an emphasis on materiality—the relationship with traditional types and topography, still a key question for Chilean architecture.[24]

Auguste Perret's visit to Buenos Aires, in 1936, had consolidated the line of a profoundly conservative, balanced and austere southern modernism, in which material and climatic conditions played a decisive part in the abstract definition of its syntagma. The aesthetic inflection in the modulation of Alberto Prebisch's house for Vicente Lopez (1937), conceived as a meticulous exercise in style and translation, and the compositional rigor, functional precision and formal and typological investigation of the house that Antonio Vilar designed for himself at San Isidro (1937) illustrate some of the principles that typify *porteño* modernism. The River Plate region was, in addition, a fertile land of exile for Antoni Bonet, one of the founders of the Grupo Austral in 1937 (along with, among others, Jorge Ferrari Hardoy and Juan Kurchan, who had got to know one another working in Le Corbusier's Parisian studio) and author, in 1953, of the well-known Casa Oks at Martínez. As has been pointed out, the combination of industrial components for dry construction (metal sections, sheet metal, various types of glass) with craft materials and methods that recalled popular skills created, in his works, contrasts of meaning characteristic of surrealist aesthetics. The Catalan architect spent the years from 1945 to 1948 in Uruguay. He became part of the cultural milieu of Montevideo, establishing ties of collaboration and friendship with the architect Julio

Vilamajó, whose residence on Calle Cullen (1930) had provided a fine example of the eclectic and innovative way in which the modern had been embraced in these intellectual circles. Bonet also frequented the sculptor Joaquín Torres Garcia, the Spanish writer Rafael Alberti (for whom he designed La Gallarda in 1945) and the young engineer Eladio Dieste, who did the calculations for the brick vaults of Casa Berlingieri (1946). In step with the local architectural debate, engaged in the definition of a "qualified modernity" that explored the *genius loci* of its own region with nostalgia, idealizing the rural world, Bonet produced numerous works dealing with the relationship of the modern with tradition and the landscape, achieving particularly interesting results in the Hostería La Solana del Mar (1947) at Punta Ballenas. It was in this period that he designed his own home, La Rinconada (1948), set on a base of rustic stone, with white plastered walls and metal uprights that support the flat roof slab. And in 1946, while Vilamajó was building Villa Serrana (a resort where nature and the primitive formed the leitmotiv of the plan), Bonet received a visit from Richard Neutra, who showed a particular interest in his Uruguayan works.[25] The following year, Marcel Breuer came to Argentina and constructed, along with Eduardo Catalano and Horacio Caminos, a small *parador*, or hotel, at Mar del Plata. Like Walter Gropius, who at the beginning of the decade had attempted to set up a professional studio in Buenos Aires, Breuer had experimented, in the house he built for himself in Lincoln (1939–40), with the possibility of combining vernacular solutions (utilizing stone walls and the technique of the balloon frame). In fact it has to be remembered that, from the forties on, with the interruption of communications with Europe as a result of the war, daily life in the Latin American countries came increasingly under the sway of the American way of life; thus there were growing ties with North American culture, which in the meantime had given refuge to many prominent figures in the European architectural debate.[26]

The research carried out in the field of the detached house in the United States acted as a magnet for the designs of the period, which found numerous formulations, especially in Frank Lloyd Wright's organicism and Neutra's residential projects on the West Coast, that were suited to making such design needs compatible: coherence and compositional fragmentation, transparence and tectonics, material and spatiality, artificiality and wilderness. Among the many possible examples in the whole Latin American area, it is worth mentioning Enrique del Moral's house at Tacubaya (1949) and, above all, Francisco Artigas's Casa del Risco at San Angel, Mexico City (1952), which was inspired by Kaufman House (Palm Springs, 1946) and became the model for the so-called

Lúcio Costa, Casa Saavedra Correias, Petrópolis, Brazil, 1942.
Lina Bo Bardi, Casa de Vidro ("Glass House"), Morumbi, São Paulo, Brazil, 1949–51.
Cristián Valdés, Casa Valdés, Santiago, Chile, 1966–67.

Oscar Niemeyer, Casa das Canoas, São Conrado, Rio de Janeiro, Brazil, 1952–53.

"El Pedregal style" (as well as the emblem of the exhibition "Latin American Architecture since 1945," organized by Henry-Russell Hitchcock at New York's Museum of Modern Art in 1955), or the nearby house of Augusto H. Alvarez which, in 1961, reinterpreted the Miesian prototype of the house-pavilion. On the East Coast, the residential works of Marcel Breuer (in a sequence of design that runs from Robinson House, 1946–48, to Hooper House, 1959) and José Luis Sert (with his home in Cambridge laid out around a series of courtyards, 1958) constituted another important group of references. The organic brand of modernism would find other declinations, depending on circumstances and international exchanges: from a rooting in the landscape of the North American kind, in which a fusion of work and nature is pursued, to the biological structuralism of Italian origin, which influenced one sector of Argentinean architectural research in those years. While "regionalisms" established and differentiated themselves in the various Latin American countries after the middle of the twentieth century, there would be points of confluence and independence in the reflections that characterized the architectural debate in the respective capitals. Thus, the centrality of the concept of space, fostered by contemporary experiences in abstract art and the theories of Bruno Zevi, would give rise to rigorous experiments in the Southern Cone in which many of these themes were brought together. The houses of Jorge Vivanco, Eduardo Sacriste and Wladimiro Acosta, in Argentina, indicate a rationalization and radicalization of the postulates that brought the very rules of the discipline into question, while Amancio Williams was able to give concrete expression to his refined technical imagination in the Casa del Arroyo at Mar del Plata (1943–45).[27]

An alternative basis for a new approach to design lay in a return to the primitive constructions of ancient America. An approach that, as is well known, would find its most significant manifestations in the art and architecture of Mexico. It suffices to recall Max Cetto's house in the gardens of El Pedregal (1949), a "mestizo" work that, with its expressive force, bears witness to the impact of the landscape, climate and Central American culture on the architect's avant-garde stock in trade; or Juan O'Gorman's house in San Jerónimo (1949) which, created out of a lava cave, would lead to the disintegration of the stylistic features of rationalism, bringing out the expressionistic and organic vein of the Mexican architect, painter and sculptor, in all its "fantastic" radicalism.[28]

In a quite different way, similar anthropological interests emerge in the research into the material vestiges of the northwest Argentina carried out by Eduardo Sacriste, and in the stone and adobe house built at Santiago in Chile by Duhart

Antonio Vilar, Casa Vilar, San Isidro, Buenos Aires, Argentina, 1937.

Julio Vilamajó, Casa Vilamajó, Montevideo, Uruguay, 1930.

Antoni Bonet, Casa Berlingieri, Punta Ballena, Maldonado, Uruguay, 1946.
Enrique del Moral, Casa del Moral, Tacubaya, Mexico, 1949.
Francisco Antigas, Casa del Risco, San Angel, Mexico City, Mexico, 1952.
Augusto H. Alvarez, Casa Alvarez, San Angel, Mexico City, Mexico, 1961.

Carlos Raúl Villanueva, Casa Sotavento, Caraballeda, Venezuela, 1957–58.
Joaquín Torres Garcia, *América*, sketch, 1936.

and Valdés in 1941. This approach to design would be taken up again in the sixties by Christian de Groote, with his house at Providencia (1961), where the dwelling is conceived as a cell of the urban fabric in which the modern enters into tension with the traditional patio typology, as well as in Cristián Valdés's house (1966–67), also in Santiago, a product of the experimental climate that then held sway in the Valparaiso school of architecture.

As many writings have shown, from different perspectives and supported by the theoretical reflections of the principal Latin American architects, the quest for an "appropriate" architecture was a shared concern, and one that played an ever greater part in the debate of the fifties and sixties, when it easily fell into line with international "rules": rules which could be followed without the need for a technically advanced construction industry (with the call for *art brut*, for the use of traditional building methods, for "truthful" materials). Producing, as a result, contributions of great quality in the ambit of neo-brutalism: it suffices to think of the expressive possibilities displayed by the Paulista movement led by João Vilanova Artigas and continued by Paulo Mendes da Rocha in his house in São Paulo (1964–66)—a paradigm both of constructional and structural rigor and of flexibility in the functional definition of its internal spaces—as well as by individual architects like Clorindo Testa in Argentina or Abraham Zabludovsky and Teodoro González de León in Mexico.[29] In this way, the most significant figures in contemporary Latin American architecture were able, starting out from the scale of the house, to investigate the potentialities of reinforced concrete and craft techniques of masonry (left visible or plastered) that did not require high levels of skill from the workforce, combining wholly personal interpretations with ideas drawn from their own cultural contexts. An example that immediately springs to mind is Luis Barragán's house at Tacubaya (1947–49), masterpiece and extreme compendium of the themes that distinguished his poetics: introspection and hierarchy of domestic rituality, compression and expansion of space, masterly composition of abstract planes and colonial walls in vibrant tints, light, color and shade to define atmospheres of intense intimacy. Finally, Mario Pani, in the house at Acapulco (1950), Carlos Raúl Villanueva, in Casa Sotavento at Caraballeda (1957–58), Eladio Dieste, in his home at Punta Gorda (1963) and Rogelio Salmona in Casa Amaral (1968), just to cite the best-known names. But also Joaquim Guedes in Brazil, Mario Paysee Reyes in Uruguay and Ernesto Katzenstein and Horacio Baliero in Argentina. All found a way to reconcile their own modernist propensities with local circumstances through sophisticated expedients of design.[30]

Despite the many missed opportunities that characterized the course of the architectural debate on the subcontinent in the closing decades of the twentieth century—a period tragically marked by military dictatorships and repeated economic crises, as well as by the devastating spread of "postmodernisms" in the cities of Latin America—this phase has led to a profound critical revision of the modern legacy and its most significant manifestations, focusing attention on urban quality and on making the most of the architectural heritage, and revealing, in the best cases, a pragmatic consolidation of professional maturation.[31] The noblest and most fertile aspects of this summarily outlined general picture still seem vital. They represent, for the new generations of Latin American architects, a common horizon against which, inevitably, they define themselves, underscoring similarities and distances through the instruments of design.

Globalization and Experimentalisms:
Conditions of Possibility

Reflection of a difficult reality, where the violence and iniquity of the suburbs coexist with the comfort and sophistication of the elite, the Latin American city is today afflicted by a process of social decay that has a direct effect on the urban fabric. The impossibility of reconciling these extremes seems to be inherent in its structure and this postulate offers a key to interpretation of the houses that, come what may, will have to reckon with this situation. There is no doubt that architecture is part of this "stratifying machinery," which produces new frontiers that are not rooted in the territory, but in the unequal distribution of consumer goods.[32] It has to be admitted, in fact, that the works we present here, located in more or less segregated residential districts, amount at times to outright "simulacra of a utopia" within the urban chaos, or find refuge in unspoiled natural settings, far from the pollution of the city. Under these privileged conditions, with a cultured and sophisticated cognitive system, they measure themselves against the "image" of the city or a substantially aestheticized landscape. While it is obvious that these outstanding "one-off pieces" can be seen as evidence of a dramatic impossibility for Latin American architecture—that of bringing about a transformation in the quality of the region's cities, devastated by unchecked processes of growth—it is equally true that they remain valid opportunities for inquiry and interpretation.[33] Although evident technological limitations persist, to a degree that varies from one country to another, as far the "housing question" is concerned this problem is certainly a relative one in the cases presented here, given the financial resources of the individual clients. Along with adaptation to the context, this

theme becomes one of the many incentives for formulations that certainly find valid antecedents in the local tradition of the modern.[34] In this way, the recourse to residential typologies that are widespread in the region concerned, the revival of craft techniques that have to be saved from oblivion, the desire to adopt ancestral methods of construction and the use of stone from quarries located faraway in the south, along with wood and thatch from forests, simple brick or reinforced concrete, constitute legitimate stimuli to design; a design which, in many cases, is committed to restoring a poetical and ritual dimension to architecture. None of this impedes an attention to the detail, the utilization of standardized building solutions or research into new materials and innovative systems of construction that will be more environmentally friendly. In each design, these architectural elements are accurately identified, reworked with cultured references drawn from the tradition of the discipline and brought up to date through differentiated languages, which often contaminate one another. The adoption of a minimalist repertoire seems, at times, particularly suited to expressing the essential and tangible values considered "typical" of Latin American culture. In other cases it is the context that suggests the codes needed for the definition of grammars more inclined to incorporate the signs and affinities of a highly characterized emotional universe. On many occasions, the designs exploit magnificent panoramas, weighing up alternative compositional responses: organic and comfortable refuges set in the rock; disjointed and centrifugal geometries, which blend into the ground and seek to reduce the impact on the surface; morphologies that stem from the laws of topography or climate; suggestive promenades that culminate in the dialectical contrast of glass pavilions suspended in the vegetation of the forest or of lakes, with recurrent allusions to the myth of Arcadia. Sometimes, the abstraction, the precision of the volumes, the simplicity and polychromy of the materials and the syntactic rejection of more elementary questions achieve original results from the typological, linguistic, compositional or spatial viewpoint. By strengthening the positive aspects of the relationship with the site (through the structure, the layout and the functional organization), contending with the desert climate of the Andean cordillera or with the intense light of the equator (in the design of doors and windows and of external devices of control), creating protective enclosures or ambiguous zones of transition between outside and inside (through varied sequences of porches and courtyards), the fleeting and precarious pact that these works of architecture reach with a boundless nature is reaffirmed. As has been observed, the modern fascination with the *tabula rasa* acquires an exponential value in Latin

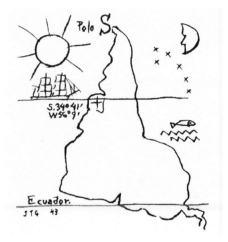

Amancio Williams, Casa del Arroyo, Mar del Plata, Argentina, 1943–45.

Luis Barragán, Casa Barragán, Tacubaya, Mexico City, Mexico, 1947–49.
Eladio Dieste, Casa Dieste, Punta Gorda, Montevideo, Uruguay, 1963.

America. In fact the grand scale is an omnipresent parameter, imposed by an extreme geography: the vast expanse of the desert or the pampas, the silence and the solitude become conditions charged with meaning. The insistence on colors, shadows and textures, on degrees of transparence and opacity, the horizontal organization of the proportions as an evocation of peace and eternity and the accentuation of compositional tensions as a tactic of resistance to the inclemency of nature are stratagems of design that are often used in a judicious manner. However, the remote places in which the works are located have now lost their "marginality." The periphery no longer has "one" center and this multiplication of the places in which things "happen" has made possible continual exchanges of ideas and experiences, flows of information that reach every corner of the planet, changing forever the coordinates in which young Latin American architects operate. With only a few exceptions (and it is no coincidence that Paulo Mendes da Rocha belongs to another generation), these are essentially pragmatic and versatile works of architecture, ready to divest themselves of a priori certainties that would limit their capacity for continual reformulation, indispensable for the rapid adaptation to requirements that the market demands from the architect today. Works that fit into a "practice" whose conceptual net oscillates between the traditional principles of the discipline and the new dynamics that affect the profession. Convinced of the futility of tracing a map of the specificities, but conscious that, in the age of cultural nomadism, the formal choices have, in the respective "code of territoriality," a trademark that labels them as "product."

On first impression, therefore, these detached houses could be built anywhere, with identical results. On closer examination, however, as has been pointed out for Casa Ixtapa, the reality is that they are highly specific objects, as much the fruit of the context as of a curious cosmopolitan vision that seems to be the distinctive trait of many of these creations.[35] Even from this point of view, in fact, they fall perfectly within their own disciplinary tradition.

As has been shown many times, through multiple strategies and conceptual systems, the recognition of the architectural solutions, building techniques and materials of a chosen and "constructed" tradition has been a constant and inclusive tendency in the Latin American architectural debate of the twentieth century, as theorization of a hypothetical alternative to the diffusion of international models. These cultural impulses have found a particularly effective representation of the demand for cultural independence that has been a mark of this century in Joaquín Torres Garcia's upside-down map (*América*, 1936). But above all, the Uruguayan artist's drawing still conveys with extreme lucidity the need for the breaking down of historically settled mental schemes, as an indispensable condition of looking at this continent from a different perspective. If it is clear that this is a "boundless" territory, in which every impression has been systematically erased, as the dizzy pace of globalization bears witness, for young Latin American architects the "non-place" is now an existential condition. Their proposals no longer require a hypothetical centrality that has now definitively dissolved into the plurality of media of the occasions that will supply, case by case, the gestures and themes necessary to the definition of the work. In this logic, architecture takes on the role of a "means of translation" of the conditions contingent on any exercise of design. Thus—in the ambit of the modern concept of "transculturation"—Latin American production could still find, in the purified strategy of "hybridization," a way of constructing unheard-of possibilities.[36]

Paraphrasing Antonio Tabucchi, every story is a game that always has its reverse. A game in which "all its variations, all the surprises, risks and audacities, blaze trails that lead toward a final objective, toward the identification of a *contradictory unity*." In the vicissitudes of contemporary architecture too, there is never a definitive moment in which *les jeux sont faits*. And so, in this case—as in the *juego del revés* that children used to chant in the courtyards of Buenos Aires—we are always ready to start over when looking at the new architecture of Latin America. Perhaps, on closing this book, the reader will have the sensation that "everything can carry on from another end and what I am writing now can start again in another way."[37]

Notes

1 Cf. Fernando Chueca Goitia, *Invariantes en l'Arquitectura hispanoamericana*, Madrid 1979. For an overview of the history of the Latin American countries, see Tulio Halperín Donghi, *The Contemporary History of Latin America*, Durham 1993 (with ample bibliography).
2 The beginning of the millennium seems to have opened a new phase in the erratic processes of democratization of Latin America, where the failure of the ultraliberalism of the nineties has led to a new wave of nationalistic populism, led by people like Hugo Chávez in Venezuela, Evo Morales in Bolivia and Néstor Kirchner in Argentina, as well as a series of unprecedented political experiences like those of Lula da Silva in Brazil, Tabaré Vazquez in Uruguay and Michelle Bachelet in Chile, alongside the emergence of figures like Ollanta Humala in Peru and López Obrador in Mexico. A "pragmatic" left that, with many nuances and differentiations, is tending to set aside ideology and adopt "orthodox" and dynamic economic policies that have resulted in high levels of growth.
3 Discarding the objective of a detailed reconstruction of the different disciplinary situations, an undertaking that would go well beyond the intentions of a publication whose essential aim is to present current trends in Latin American architecture to the general public, it seems more appropriate to provide the reader with the pertinent bibliographic titles. For an overall assessment of the Latin American historiographical debate and the questionable ways in which a significant section of European critics has tackled the subject, see Mercedes Daguerre, "Eladio Dieste: peripezie storiografiche," in Mercedes Daguerre (ed.), *Eladio Dieste 1917– 2000*, Milan 2003, pp. 6–17 (with ample bibliography).

4 The peripheral status, as an additional conditioning on operators in the continual tension between these polarities (a consequence of the coexistence of two radically contrasting societies, the elite and the marginal sectors), has been interpreted by Liernur in terms of what Lévi-Strauss calls "savage thinking." Thus it is the *bricoleur*, the person who uses whatever means are at hand, who, expressing himself through "mythic thought," uses the "sign" to act on the world: "[...] so he operates in a closed pragmatic universe in which the rule of his game is always that of making do with what he has. The range of means used by the *bricoleur* cannot be defined, therefore, through a project, but only by its instruments [...]. Quite apart from the recognition of the brilliant and unexpected results to which the mechanism of 'savage thinking' can lead, it is clear that in a situation dominated by 'scientific thinking' it will be difficult for the modern peripheral *bricoleur* to escape from the circle of domination: this is true when, believing himself to be operating on the dominant side, he in reality places himself on the opposite one, not being able to 'open up,' but only to 'reorganize,' and when, laying claim to an autonomous liberating project, he professes to remain in the illusorily original and genuine field of mythic thought, without realizing the profound and insurmountable contradiction between the two, in that it is precisely the notion of project that constitutes the foundation of the system that he wants to bring into question." Cf. Jorge F. Liernur, *America Latina. Architettura, gli ultimi vent'anni*, Milan 1990, pp. 9, 30–31.
5 On the concept of globalization as a "set of processes of homogenization and, at the same time, fragmentation of the world, which rearranges differences and inequalities without eliminating them," see Néstor García Canclini, *La globalización imaginada*, Mexico City-Buenos Aires-Barcelona 1999, p. 49; on the subject see too Lawrence Grossberg, "Cultural Studies, Modern Logics, and Theories of Globalisation," in Angela McRobbie (ed.), *Back to Reality: Social Experience and Cultural Studies*, Manchester 1997. These reflections should be placed in a perspective in which the concept of "multiculturalism" presupposes the acceptance of diversity, while "interculturalism" implies that "diversity develops as such in relations of negotiation, conflict and mutual borrowing"; cf. Néstor García Canclini, *Diferentes, desiguales y desconectados. Mapas de la interculturalidad*, Barcelona 2004, p. 15.
6 It is predictable that, considering the great crisis of 2001–02 and notwithstanding the encouraging signs of recovery, the difficult economic situation of the Latin American countries should have a heavy influence on investment in building and the adoption of social policies in the areas of housing and urban services, limiting the resources available for culture and research. On the other hand, the possibility of embarking on one's career much earlier than in the developed countries and therefore of having a substantial body of works constructed after just a few years of professional practice, the low costs of building owing to the lack of union protection for the workforce and the flexibility or absence of building standards and regulations which permit an experimentation that is often hampered by more rigid and bureaucratized systems of control, together with a strong European cultural imprinting, are some of the "specific" conditions of the profession of architecture in Latin America. Themes that were tackled in the debate held on October 8, 2004, at the Catholic University of Santiago in Chile and reported in Fabrizio Gallanti, Francisca Insulza (eds.), "Esiste un'identità dell'architettura latinoamericana?" *Domus*, no. 875, November 2004, pp. 82–87.
7 For a precise reconstruction of the superimposition of architectural models from the various traditions of the modern in the Latin American detached house, see Carlos E. Días Comas, Miquel Adrià, *La casa latinoamericana moderna. 20 paradigmas de mediados del siglo XX*, Mexico City-Barcelona 2003.
8 As Liernur has shown, the Argentina of Wladimiro Acosta, the Brazil of Gregori Warchavchik and the California of Rudolph Schindler and Richard Neutra are fascinating places to look for the influence of the avant-garde myth of the "noble savage." The subject has been discussed in *Wladimiro Acosta*, Buenos Aires 1988, in particular pp. 18–29; see too, *Monte Verità*, Milan 1978. A cultural stereotype that is still current in the Italian debate, in which excellent opportunities to get to know the architecture of Latin America evaporate in frivolous quests for "marvelous alternatives"; on the subject see Mercedes Daguerre, *Eladio Dieste: peripezie storiografiche*, cit., in particular pp. 10 ff.
9 Specific solutions in relation to the climate, the originality of the structural definition, monumentality as a means of asserting a new conception of city planning, the artistic contribution of the landscaping of Roberto Burle Marx and the murals of Candido Portinari are traits that were to become distinctive and recurrent in twentieth-century Brazilian architecture. On the subject see Carlos A. Ferreira Martins, "Construir una arquitectura, construir un país," in *Brasil 1920–1950. De la antropogafia a Brasilia*, Valencia 2000, pp. 371–429. On the "synthesis of the arts" as a topos that recurs in the most significant examples of Latin American architecture, see Carlos Brillembourg (ed.), *Latin American Architecture 1929–1960. Contemporary Reflections*, New York 2004.
10 As is well known, reflections on the neocolonial caught the interest of many Latin American intellectuals, artists and architects of the period, including Lúcio Costa in Brazil (one of the founders, in 1938, of the Serviço do Patrimônio Histórico e Artístico Nacional), Antonio Vilar in Argentina and Carlos Obregón Santacilia and Luis Barragán in Mexico, to mention just a few. On the theme see *Brasil 1920–1950...*, cit., and Jorge F. Liernur, *Arquitectura en la Argentina del siglo XX. La construcción de la modernidad*, Buenos Aires 2001, in particular pp. 138–63. The texts cited offer an ample bibliography on the neocolonial movement in Latin America.
11 The periodical Seminars on Latin American Architecture (SAL) which have been held at various academic centers on the continent since 1985 have endorsed an approach based on conservation, environmentalism and the attempt to define a "national identity." A discourse that, forgetting the operations of selection and mixture that lie at the base of the distinctive characteristics of its culture, has sought to sanction a fictitious "unity" for the whole continent, relativizing the differences through the standardization of its most significant figures. On this see Mercedes Daguerre, "Eladio Dieste: peripezie storiografiche...," cit., pp. 6–17. More up-to-date researches have tried to shift the attention from the question of identity to that of intercultural diversity; on these themes see David T. Goldberg (ed.), *Multiculturalism: A Critical Reader*, Cambridge (MA)-Oxford 1994.
12 Among the numerous writings on Le Corbusier's troubled experience in Latin

America and the influence of his 1929 visit on his subsequent theoretical ideas, we refer the reader to: Cecila Rodrigues dos Santos et al., *Le Corbusier e o Brasil*, São Paulo 1987; Carlos A. Ferreira Martins, "État, nature et culture. Le Corbusier et Lucio Costa aux origines de l'architecture moderne au Brésil," in *Le Corbusier et la Nature*, Paris 1991; Carlos E. Días Comas, *Le Corbusier y Sudamérica: viajes y proyectos*, Santiago 1991; Idem, *Le Corbusier e Rio*, Rio de Janeiro 1999; Kenneth Frampton, "Le Corbusier and Oscar Niemeyer: Influence and Counterinfluence, 1929–1965," in Carlos Brillembourg (ed.), *Latin American Architecture 1929–1960. Contemporary Reflections*, London 2000, pp. 34–49; Collins Craseman, "Le Corbusier's Maison Errázuriz: A conflict of Fictive Cultures," in *Harvard Architectural Review*, no. 6, 1987; Jorge F. Liernur, "Pablo Pschepiurca, Precisiones sobre los proyectos de Le Corbusier en la Argentina 1929–1949," in *Summa*, no. 243, November 1987, pp. 40–55; Jorge F. Liernur, *Arquitectura en la Argentina del Siglo XX. La construcción de la modernidad...*, cit., in particular pp. 167 ff.; Jorge F. Liernur, *Précisions* (in course of publication).

13 On the subject, cf. Jorge F. Liernur, "Un nuovo mondo per lo spirito nuovo: le scoperte dell'America Latina da parte della cultura architettonica del XX secolo," in *Zodiac*, no. 8, 1992–93, pp. 84–121; Bernd Nicolai (ed.), *Architektur und Exil: Kulturtransfer, Emigration und Exil in der Moderne 1930–1950*, Trier 2003; Susanne Dussel, *Max Cetto (1903–1980). Arquitecto mexicano alemán*, Mexico City 1995. It should be remembered, too, that Hans Schmidt was also interested in this "new world," designing a semidetached house in Mexico City in 1929. On Luis Barragán's relations with Max Cetto (a pupil of Hans Poelzig

and assistant of Ernst May in Frankfurt who left Germany in 1937 and moved to Mexico in 1939, after working in Richard Neutra's studio in California) and Mathias Goeritz (who arrived in Guadalajara in 1949 to teach at the local school of architecture) see Adrián Gorelik, Jorge F. Liernur, *La sombra de la vanguardia. Hannes Meyer en México 1938–1949*, Buenos Aires 1993, in particular pp. 102 ff.

14 It is symptomatic that the internationalist convictions expressed by O'Gorman in 1932, which Meyer criticized in 1939, were inspired by radical positions similar to those held by Meyer in his Soviet period. Thus Meyer called for a return to national traditions of construction instead of the reinforced concrete utilized by Mexican functionalist architects, recanting—in accord with the official political line of the construction of socialism in a single country—the cosmopolitanism he had proclaimed in 1926. In the tradition of the generic "return to the origins" that accompanied the processes of change triggered by the crisis of 1929, it was the originality of Hannes Meyer's regionalist proposal that made him a credible interlocutor within a discussion that had already gotten under way at the beginning of the decade, when, breaking with certain modernist premises and through a similar shift toward regionalism, one sector of Mexican architectural radicalism had taken on the agrarian challenge of Cardenism. For O'Gorman, in fact, it was the typology and not the image of the Mexican *jacal* that constituted a valid model of reference for a rational architecture that had to tackle the question of low-cost housing in a scientific way; a position relativized in other proposals of the period, in which an attempt was made to revive, through the language, the "charm" of the rural dwelling. Cf. Adrián Gorelik, Jorge F. Lier-

nur, *La sombra de la vanguardia. Hannes Meyer en México 1938–1949...* cit., in particular pp. 15–67; on the question see too José Antonio Aldrete-Haas, "The Search for Roots in Mexican Modernism," in Carlos Brillembourg (ed.), *Latin American Architecture 1929–1960...*, cit., pp. 100–15. On Frida Kahlo and Diego Rivera's house-studio, cf. Luis E. Carranza, "Contemplando la razón. Juan O'Gorman e la dialettica dell'architettura moderna," in *Casabella*, no. 689, May 2001, pp. 8–21. The episode is revealing of the wide variety of inflections that the relationship between tradition and the modern took on in the Latin American architectural debate of the twentieth century.

15 Born in Odessa, Warchavchik graduated from the Istituto di Belle Arti in Rome and arrived in Brazil in 1923. Delegate for South America at the 3rd CIAM in Brussels (1930), he tackled the numerous cultural and technical difficulties entailed in the adoption of the "rationalist doctrine" in tropical countries. Among his early works, it is worth mentioning the house on Calle Itápolis, in São Paulo, visited by Le Corbusier in 1929 while it was under construction, or Casa Nordchild in Rio de Janeiro, inaugurated in 1931 in the presence of Frank Lloyd Wright, who was in the city of the Cariocas at the time as an additional member of the jury of the international competition for the Columbus Lighthouse. In 1932 Warchavchik went into partnership with Lúcio Costa and the young Oscar Niemeyer worked with them. The construction of the workers' houses at Gamboa brought their collaboration to an end. On Warchavchik's work see, in addition to the texts already cited, *Gregori Warchavchik*, exhibition catalogue, São Paulo 1981.

16 As demonstrated by recent studies, not all the rationalist research of the period was

carried out under the indisputable influence of Le Corbusier: Paulo de Camargo y Almeida, Paulo Antunes Ribeiro and Attilio Correa Lima constructed works of quality with a wide range of references to the avant-garde and, in the case of the work of Luiz Nunez, a different relationship was established between modern design and historical heritage than the one that held sway in the forties. On the architects cited see Carlos A. Ferreira Martins, "Construir una arquitectura, construir un país," cit. On Rino Levi's work in São Paulo cf.: Renato Anelli et al., *Rino Levi. Arquitetura and cidade*, São Paulo 2001; Renato Anelli, "Rino Levi. Mediterraneo ai tropici. Trasformazioni del patio mediterraneo nell'architettura moderna brasiliana," in *Casabella*, no. 708, February 2003, pp. 86–95.

17 Giedion was aware of the difficulty of explaining the development of modernism in Brazil simply in terms of relationships of "influence"; cf. Sigfried Giedion, "Brazil and Contemporary Architecture," preface to Henrique Mindlin, *Modern Architecture in Brazil*, New York 1956 (French ed., Paris 1956; German ed., Munich 1956; Portuguese ed., Rio de Janeiro 1999), pp. 17–18. For an analysis of Giedion's considerations, see Carlos A. Ferreira Martins, "Construir una arquitectura, construir un país," cit. As is well known, following the exhibition held at MoMA and the publication of Goodwin's book (Philip E. Goodwin, *Brazil Builds. Architecture New and Old, 1652–1942*, New York 1943), numerous specialist magazines showed an interest in Brazilian modernism, including: *The Architectural Record*, vol. 95, March 1944; *Architectural Forum*, November 1947; *L'Architecture d'aujord'hui*, no. 13–14, September 1947 and no. 42–43, August 1952.

18 At the very moment of greatest international consensus, when modern

Brazilian architecture began to be seen as a genuine "national style," a controversy sprang up over the visit to Brazil by Sigfried Giedion, Walter Gropius, Alvar Aalto, Ernesto Nathan Rogers and Max Bill, on the occasion of the São Paulo Biennale of Architecture in 1953. The positions of the critics then became polarized between admiration of the originality of Brazilian architecture and the accusation of a "betrayal" of the social postulates of the modern orthodoxy. A paradox that was made even more glaring by the contradiction that it had been an authoritarian state which had adopted modern architecture as its official style in its ideological efforts to construct a national identity (a task undertaken by Lúcio Costa, on the theoretical plane, and by the talented architects of the "Carioca group," led by Oscar Niemeyer, on that of design). The debate reached its climax in "Report on Brazil," published in *The Architectural Review*, vol. 114, July 1953, pp. 234–50. On the mode of construction of the "case" of Brazil in the historiography of modern architecture, see the contributions by Carlos Ferreira Martin and Ana M. Rigotti in "Brasil," *Block*, no. 4, 1999, pp. 8–22, 78–86.

19 The literature on the subject is very extensive; in addition to the titles already cited, we refer the reader to some recent researches: Zilah Quezado Deckker, *Brazil Built: The Architecture of the Modern Movement in Brazil*, London 2001; Carlos E. Días Comas, "Rapport du Brésil," in J.-F. Lejeune (ed.), *Cruauté et utopie, villes et paysages d'Amérique latine*, Brussels 2003, pp. 173–80; Adrian Forty, Elisabetta Andreoli (eds.), *Brazil's Modern Architecture*, London 2004.

20 On the subject, cf. Carlos A. Ferreira Martins, "Construir una arquitectura, construir un país," cit., in particular pp.

375–76; Adrián Gorelik, "Tentativas de comprender una ciudad moderna," in Carlos Ferreira Martin, Ana M. Rigotti "Brasil," cit., pp. 62–76. As is well-known, the revolution led by Getúlio Vargas, in 1930, installed a government with strongly nationalistic aspirations, ratified in 1937 with the proclamation of the Estado Novo, which would find in modern architecture the answer to its symbolic needs, as well as an effective means of national unification. On this see Carlos A. Ferreira Martins, *Arquitectura e Estado no Brasil. Elementos para a constituição do discurso moderno no Brasil*, São Paulo 1987. The theoretical construction of Lúcio Costa, consolidated in the dominant historiographical analysis, is made clear in *Razões da Nova Arquitectura* (1934); *Documentação Necessári* (1938); *Depoimento de um Arquitecto carioca* (1951); all published in Lúcio Costa, *Registro de uma Vivência*, São Paulo 1995. On Costa's work see too Guilherme Wisnik, *Lúcio Costa*, São Paulo 2001 (with ample bibliography).

21 As has been pointed out several times, it was in the construction of a new type of state that modernism found, in Latin America, an unprecedented field of action to try out new registers and declinations. Mexico, Brazil, Venezuela and Argentina were all chapters in a modernization that, in its attempt to overcome an accentuated social, ethnical and territorial fragmentation, has produced highly characterized urban settings and works of architecture, in which the role of the public sector has been that of promoting innovation, seeking to give itself a strong charge representative of its role of transformation. A tendency still at work in the fifties and sixties, it would progressively fade with the emergence of new laissez-faire policies in which the very notion of

"development" seems to have been emptied of all significance. The theme of the relationship between modernity and state, in the various countries of Latin America, has been tackled on many occasions; in addition to the titles already cited, we refer readers looking for a concise overview to Adrián Gorelik, "Nostalgia y plan: el estado como vanguardia," in Gustavo Curiel et al. (eds.), *Arte, historia e identidad en América. Visiones comparativas*, vol. II, Mexico City 1994.

22 For a thorough analysis of the critical reception given to Brasilia, see Adrián Gorelik, "Tentativas de comprender una ciudad moderna," cit., pp. 62–76; for a placing of the experience in the more general perspective of twentieth-century architecture, cf. Manfredo Tafuri, Francesco Dal Co, *Architettura Contemporanea*, Milan 1976, pp. 342–43 (English ed., *Modern Architecture*, trans. by Robert Erich Wolf, New York 1979).

23 In this connection cf.: João Masao Kamita, "The Modern Brazilian House," in Adrian Forty, Elisabetta Andreoli (eds.), *Brazil's Modern Architecture*, cit., pp. 140–69; Carlos E. Días Comas, "La casa unifamiliar moderna. Aportaciones latinoamericanas (1915–1975)," in Carlos E. Días Comas, Miquel Adrià, *La casa latinoamericana moderna*, cit., pp. 6–27. On the work of Lina Bo Bardi, see Antonella Gallo (ed.), *Lina Bo Bardi architetto*, Venice 2004; Olivia de Oliveira, *Lina Bo Bardi. Sutis Substâncias da Arquitetura*, São Paulo-Barcelona 2005.

24 On this subject see Fernando Pérez Oyarzun, *Arquitectura moderna en Chile*, Santiago 2001. On the two currents of thought that developed in the Chilean architecture of the second half of the twentieth century (the poetic inflection of the Valparaiso school of architecture and the philosophical one of Juan Borchers),

determining its strong phenomenological propensity, see, by the same author, "Ortodossia/eterodossia. Architettura moderna in Cile," *Casabella*, no. 650, November 1997, pp. 8–13. On the relationship between architecture and location in contemporary Chilean architecture, cf. also, Horacio Torrent, "Pacto precario: cajas leves o topografias sensibles," in *2G*, no. 26, 2003, pp. 14–25.

25 It should be recalled that in 1938 Bonet had designed the famous BKF (Bonet, Kurchan, Ferrari Hardoy) chair, a manifesto of the successful organic synthesis between technology and craftsmanship. On the work of Antonio Bonet, see Fernando Alvarez, Jordi Roig, *Antoni Bonet Castellana 1913–1989*, Barcelona 1996 (with ample bibliography). For the cultural debate that went on in the forties in the River Plate area, where regionalism formed one of the different strands of the neo-humanism of Catholic origin, which reflected on the distinctive features of a modern architecture that was at the same time identified with local traditions and materials, see Jorge F. Liernur, *Arquitectura en la Argentina del siglo XX. La construcción de la modernidad*, cit., pp. 229–44; in addition, Pablo Pschepiurca, "BKF: annuncio di una nuova modernità," *Casabella*, no. 711, May 2003, pp. 106–07. On Julio Vilamajó's work and the relations between Dieste and Bonnet, in the milieu in which the Uruguayan engineer spent his formative years, see also: *Julio Vilamajó. La poetica dell'interiorità*, Naples 1998; Graciela Silvestre, "L'ornamento che custodisce il piacere," in *Casabella*, no. 697, February 2002, pp. 62–69; Idem, "Una biografia uruguaiana," in Mercedes Daguerre (ed.), *Eladio Dieste 1917–2000*, cit., pp: 18–51; Idem, "Dieste: modernità senza conflitti?" *Casabella*, no. 684–85, December 2000–

January 2001, pp. 61–87. On the work of Antonio Vilar, cf. too, Adrián Gorelik, "Antonio Vilar. Peregrinazioni del Moderno," *Casabella*, no. 695–96, December 2001–January 2002, pp. 64–73.

26 For the special relationship that the United States established in this period with the South American countries, see Jorge F. Liernur, "The South American Way," in *Brasil 1920–1950...*, cit., pp. 23–41, and Lauro Cavalcanti, "Architecture, Urbanism, and the Good Neighbor Policy: Brazil and the United States," in Carlos Brillembourg (ed.), *Latin American Architecture 1929–1960...*, cit., pp. 50–59.

27 For concise biographies of the Argentinean architects cited in this essay, we refer the reader to Fernando Aliata, Jorge F. Liernur (eds.), *Dicionario de Arquitectura en la Argentina*, Buenos Aires 2004, 6 vols.; in addition, *Amancio Williams*, Buenos Aires 1990.

28 On the Mexican houses referred to, see Carlos E. Días Comas, Miquel Adrià, *La casa latinoamericana moderna...*, cit.

29 As is well known, the shift toward the monumental theorized by Giedion, Sert and Léger with the publication of *Nine Points on Monumentality* (1943), the disputes within the CIAM and the opening of new lines of research in the international postwar debate would act as a stimulus for these developments in Latin American countries as well. The monographs cited refer to an extensive bibliography: J. Massao Kamita, *Vilanova Artigas*, São Paulo 2000; Annette Spiro, *Paulo Mendes da Rocha. Works and Projects*, Zurich 2002; Miquel Adrià, *Abraham Zabludovsky y la vivienda*, Mexico City 2000; Idem (ed.), *Teodoro González de León. Obra completa*, Mexico City 2004; Manuel Cuadra et al., *Clorindo Testa*, Rotterdam 2000.

30 As has been made clear, what European critics saw as an alternative area of

production to the International Style, represented instead, in the Latin American context, a "project of reconciliation": a series of diverse and highly realistic responses to the situation in which these architects found themselves working. Cf. Jorge F. Liernur, *America latina. Architettura, gli ultimi vent'anni*, cit., pp. 33–34. In this connection see too: Alan Colquhoun, "The concept of Regionalism," in Gülsüm Baydar Nalbantoglu, Wong Chong Thai (eds.), *Postcolonial Space(s)*, New York 1997, pp. 13–23; Kenneth Frampton, "Critical Regionalism, Modern Architecture and Cultural Identity," in Idem, *Modern Architecture: A Critical History*, London 1985. In *Studies in Tectonic Culture* (1995), Frampton goes beyond the notion of "critical regionalism," which supposed a virtual center of formulation to which local languages had to be adapted, with his thesis of the emergence of a worldwide architectural culture; on the theme, see Giovanni Leoni, review of Kenneth Frampton, *Studies in Tectonic Culture. The Poetics of Construction in Nineteenth and Twentieth Century Architecture*, Cambridge, Mass. 1995, in *Casabella*, no. 649, October 1997, pp. 87–88. Symptomatic, from this point of view, is the production of Eladio Dieste in Uruguay, Oscar Niemeyer in Brazil or Luis Barragán in Mexico. On the work of these architects, in addition to the titles already cited, we will limit ourselves to indicating the most significant contributions that offer an exhaustive bibliography: Mercedes Daguerre (ed.), *Eladio Dieste 1917–2000*, cit.; Josep Maria Botey, *Oscar Niemeyer*, Barcelona 1994; Antonio Riggen Martínez, *Luis Barragán 1902–1988*, Milan 1996.

31 This succinct survey is intended simply to register the variety of questions with which the new generations of Latin American architects have to reckon. On the developments in the architectural and urban debate in Latin America in the last decades of the twentieth century, see: Jorge F. Liernur, *America latina. Architettura, gli ultimi vent'anni*, cit.; Graciela Silvestri, Adrián Gorelik, "Ciudad y cultura urbana 1976–1999, el fin de la expansión," in José Luis Romero, Luis Alberto Romero, *Buenos Aires, historia de cuatro siglos*, Buenos Aires 2000; Hugo Segawa (ed.), *Arquiteturas no Brasil/Anos 80*, São Paulo 1998; Fernando Pérez Oyarzun, "Poéticas del caso," in *Arquitectura Viva*, no. 85, July–August 2002, pp. 28–35; Enrique de Anda, "20 anni di architettura messicana (1980–2000)," in *Casabella*, no. 703, September 2002, pp. 14–19.

32 The use of two extreme paradigms of reference in the formal articulation of the Latin American city—that of the "contaminated city," in which the leisured classes recognize the existence of poverty as an inevitable component of the urban world and seek residential alternatives in basically self-sufficient areas; and that of the "white city," where marginality is completely excluded from the enclosure that defends the otherness of the entire center, in which ideal living conditions are created—allows us to understand the general context of these detached houses. Cf. J.F. Liernur, *America Latina. Architettura, gli ultimi vent'anni*, cit., pp. 14–15. In this connection see too Alberto Sato, "Simulacros urbanos," in *Punto*, 1982; the concept of rationalist islands has been discussed by R. Lopez Rangel in Rafael López Rangel, Roberto Segre, *Tendencias arquitectónicas y caos urbano en América Latina*, Havana 1986. For an up-to-date approach to the historical debate on the Latin American city, cf. Adrián Gorelik, "A produção da 'cidade latinoamericana,'" in *Tempo Social. Re-*

vista de sociología da USP, vol. 17, no. 1, June 2005, pp. 111–33.

33 Significant, from this point of view, is the simultaneous involvement of many of these architects in innovative professional approaches to social housing (as in the case of Aravena, with the proposal advanced by Elemental, in Chile, which revives the possibility of combining a policy of low-cost construction with architectural quality) or the metropolitan dimension (for example, the scheme for the environmental rehabilitation of the catchment basin of Mexico City drawn up by Alberto Kalach or the interdisciplinary project "ZMV. Metropolitan Zone of the Valle de México" of the studio LCM/Fernando Romero). On this subject see Alejandro Aravena, "Quinta Monroy-Elemental," *Casabella*, no. 742, March 2006, pp. 83–91; in addition, Miquel Adrià, *Alberto Kalach*, Mexico City 2004, and Federica Zanco, "Architettura come sistema di traduzione," *Casabella*, no. 725, September 2004, pp. 30–32.

34 From this perspective, rather than a "reassuring hybridization" which ignores the differences that won't go away, the "modern" of reference should be understood—in the sense it is used by Garcia Canclini—as a project based on a conflicting mixture of heterogeneous memory and failure to innovate. On the theme cf. Néstor Garcia Canclini, *La globalización imaginada*, cit.

35 On the new conditions in which young Latin American architects find themselves working, see Federica Zanco, "Architettura come sistema di traduzione," cit., p. 32. On the subject see also Alberto Sato, "Trazas," *2G*, no. 8, 1998, pp. 24–29.

36 On the concept of "hybridization" in the Latin American debate of recent years, cf. Néstor Garcia Canclini, *Culturas*

híbridas. Estrategias para entrar y salir de la modernidad, Mexico City 1989. Reflections that have been extended to the field of architecture: cf. Felipe Hernández, "On the Notion of Architectural Hybridisation in Latin America," *The Journal of Architecture*, vol. 7, no. 1, April 2002, pp. 77–86; Idem, "Éspaces d'Hybridation: Les Maisons des Architectes," in J.-F. Lejeune (ed.), *Cruauté et utopie...*, cit.

37 The last two quotations are taken from José Cardoso Pires's preface to the Portuguese edition

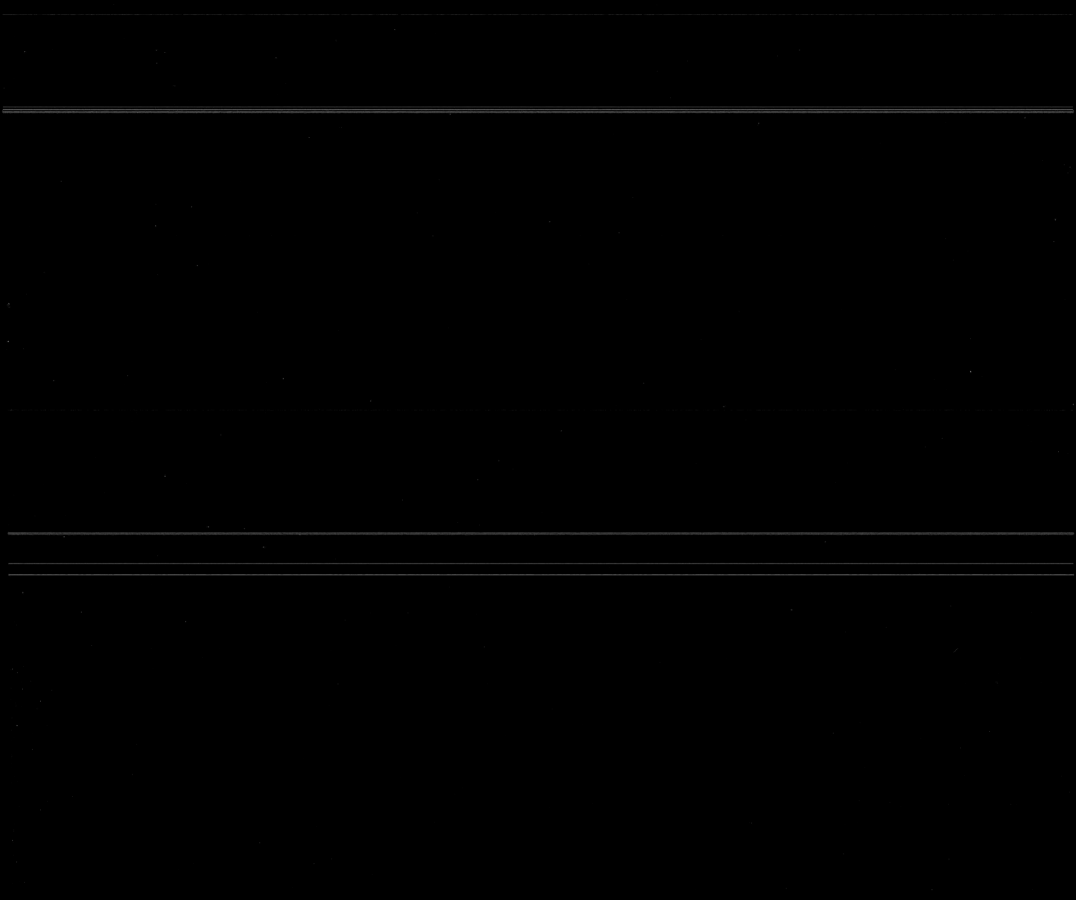

1

andrade & morettin

Vinicius Hernandes de Andrade (São Paulo, 1968) and Marcelo Morettin (São Paulo, 1969) graduated, in 1992 and 1991 respectively, from the Faculty of Architecture and City Planning at the University of São Paulo (FAUUSP). After collaborating with several well-known Brazilian architects (including Eduardo de Almeida, Joaquim Guedes and Paulo Mendes da Rocha), they have been practicing together since 1997. They have taken part in numerous competitions and have won prizes on several occasions: 4th Iberoamerican Biennial of Architecture (IAB), Lima, 2004; 6th São Paulo International Biennial, 2005; mention at the IAB "Jovens Arquitetos" in 2005. Their works have been published in well-known specialist magazines and exhibited overseas: "Jovens Arquitetos Iberoamericanos," Lisbon, 1994; 11th Congress of the International Union of Architects in Barcelona, 1996; "Brazil Still Builds—Brazilian Houses," at the Architectural Association in London, 1999; "Encore Moderne? Architecture brésilienne 1928–2005," Paris, 2005. Currently under construction in São Paulo: residential complex on Rua Aimberê, the headquarters of the Fondação do Desenvolvimento da Educação (FDE), a low-cost housing project on Rua da Assembléia and the renovation of the Faculty of Medicine of the USP.

alessandro carapicuiba's house são paulo brazil 1998

design
Vinicius Andrade,
Marcelo Morettin
collaborators
J.G. da Silveira, J.Ed. Alves
structure
ITA Construtora: Helio Olga
building contractors
J. Francisco Chaves
clients
Paulo D'Alessandro,
Domitilia Coelho
location
Carapicuiba, São Paulo, Brazil

dimensions
600 sqm site area
62 sqm built area

dates
1997: project
1998: construction

This small pavilion, designed for a young couple of photographers, is located in the environs of the metropolitan area of São Paulo, on a lot densely planted with trees and bounded by a lake to the north. The elementary structure of the house consists of two connected volumes of contrasting form and materials. The two blocks, ranged along the longitudinal axis of the site, exploit the profile of the great canopy of trees to try to install the living room in the open space comprised between the ground and the foliage. The main block, made up of a single room, is defined by a light structure of Jatoba wood, filled with panels of cellular polycarbonate that, thanks to their partial transparence, establish an evocative relationship with the surroundings. In one corner of the building, the translucent membrane gives way to the transparence of glass, framing a particular view of the lake. The room, characterized by an extreme fluidity of space and the special properties of its envelope, allows the perception of the natural landscape to be incorporated into the domestic setting, attenuating the traditional rigid separation of the private sphere. A folding blind makes it possible to isolate the night zone occasionally, introducing a dimension of time into the dwelling. For structural and compositional reasons, the box full of light has been raised above the ground on brick plinths. In a similar way, the roof, made of metal tiles fitted with thermal and acoustic insulation, is a free and inclined plane, suspended above the building, thereby preserving its volumetric integrity. The block of services contains all the house's facilities: kitchen, laundry, bathroom and tanks for the storage of water and gas. Absolutely antithetical to the main pavilion, it is conceived as a solid firmly planted on the ground, from which it rises directly with thick masonry walls, and screens the adjacent nucleus from the setting sun. The floor surfaces of the bathroom and the kitchen, as well as all the closets and internal partitions, are also in brick and concrete. The few openings are proportionate to and distributed on the basis of the function they perform, emphasizing the closed and solid image of this wing of the house in contrast to the other. The different degrees of transparence that characterize the shell of the first pavilion, reacting to variations in the light, natural as well as artificial, lead to distinct interpretations of the architectural object. At the same time, the optical distortions and ambiguities generated by the filling panels give rise to a perception of the landscape that at times invites abstraction and at others contemplation.

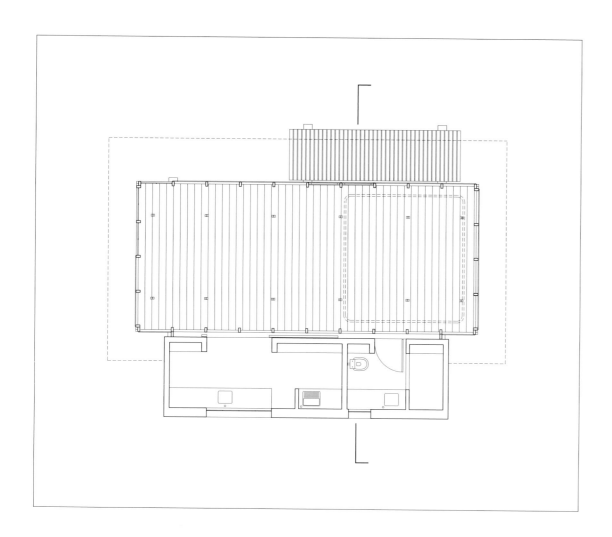

Plan.

East, north and west elevations and cross section.

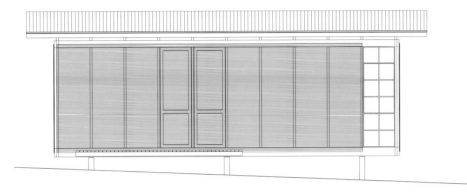

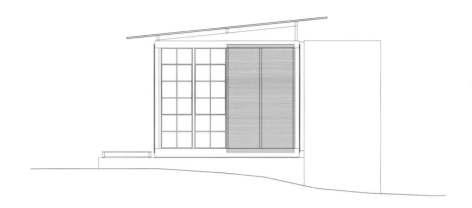

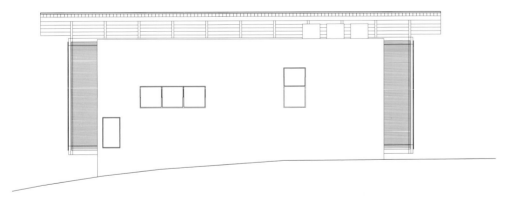

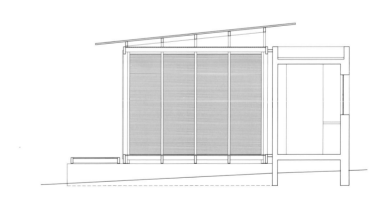

Details of the east front.

View of the house in the forest.

View of the east front.

Internal views of the day zone.

2 alejandro aravena

Alejandro Aravena (Santiago, Chile, 1967) graduated in architecture from the Pontifical Catholic University of Chile in 1992. Subsequently he studied at the School of Architecture in Venice (IUAV). In 1994 he opened his own professional studio. He has been a visiting teacher at the Architectural Association in London and at Harvard University, which staged an exhibition of his work in 2004. His work has received wide international recognition, including special mentions at the Venice Biennale and the 3rd Iberoamerican Biennial of Architecture and Engineering, finalist at the Mies van der Rohe Award for Latin America (Barcelona 2000) and first prize at the 12th Santiago Biennial in Chile. Designated the best architect "under 40" by the Chilean Association of Architects, he was also a member of the discussion group on the future development of Chile called "El Chile que viene." His works have been published in international specialist magazines, including: *Casabella*, *Arquitectura Viva*, *Arquine*, *Summa+*, *ARQ*. His most significant projects include: the house of the sculptress Francisca Cerda located in Santiago (1997), the Huelquén Montessori elementary school (2001) and the Departments of Mathematics (1998–99), Medicine (2001–04) and Architecture (2004) at the Catholic University of Chile, and a tower to house the Department of Digital Education (2003–06) at the same university; the Quinta Monroy – Elemental housing project at Iquique, Chile (2002–04), has just been completed.

house on lake pirehueico chile 2004

design
Alejandro Aravena
collaborators
Jorge Christie, Victor Oddó
structure
Félix Gutiérrez
works supervisor
Juan Antonio Navarrete
building contractors
Juan Antonio Navarrete & Co.
client
Alberto Combeau
location
Lake Pirehueico, X Región, Chile

dimensions
100,000 sqm site area
350 sqm built area

dates
2003: project
2004: construction

A virgin site in the south of Chile on which to build a vacation house. Starting out from this fact, the design is the result of an equation that takes account of all the variables present in the location: volcanic soil, intense annual rainfall, strong exposure to sunlight, winds from the north and east, view of the lake, the park and other specific points, correct heliothermic orientation, choice of the materials and the building method in relation to the house's isolated and remote location, detailed analysis of the way in which the dwelling will be utilized. At the client's explicit request, the formal response had to be a direct expression of these natural conditions, excluding a priori any aesthetic influence on the definition of the architectural language. A pragmatic approach, therefore, has guided the development of the proposal. The distinctive geometries of the second floor and the design of the windows, with very rigid frames, are explained by the desire to provide the best views and ward off the violent gusts of wind. The volumes with their uneven profile were then faced with shingles and covered with pitched roofs to cope with the abundant local rainfall. The ground floor, by contrast, is a regular and resistant box, capable of withstanding occasional earth tremors and guaranteeing adequate levels of security for a house that is left unoccupied for much of the year. The stone slabs of the facing come from nearby quarries, while the timber is the product of the partial clearing of trees from the site that the construction of the house made necessary.

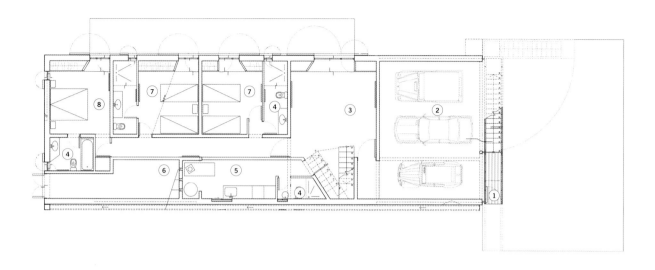

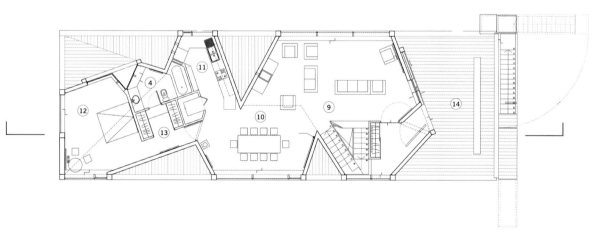

Plans of the ground and second floors. Legend 1 entrance 2 garage 3 entrance hall
4 bathroom 5 laundry 6 cellar 7 bedroom 8 double bedroom 9 living room
10 dining room 11 kitchen 12 double bedroom 13 wardrobe 14 terrace.

East and north elevations and longitudinal section.

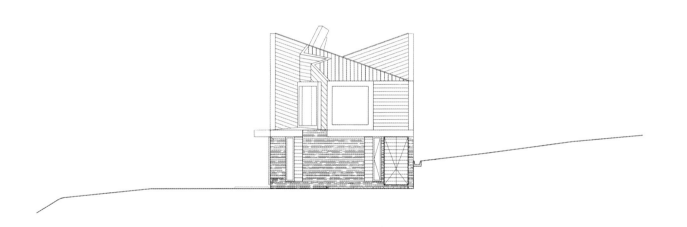

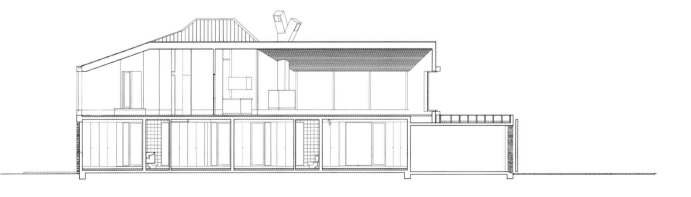

37

Study sketches and view of the east front.

View from the southeast and detail of the west front.

The relationship between the stone base and the wooden volumes on the first floor at the western corner and along the east front.

Internal views of the living room.

3 javier artadi

Javier Artadi (Lima, 1961) graduated in 1985 from the Faculty of Architecture and City Planning of the Ricardo Palma University in Lima. In 1986 he opened his own professional studio. He has won numerous competitions and his works have been given awards at the Peru Biennial of Architecture and the most recent Iberoamerican Biennial. He has staged exhibitions and given lectures in Latin America and several European countries. He is full professor of architectural design at the Peruvian University of Applied Sciences. Among his more significant works it is worth mentioning the renovation of the Etiquetas Peruanas factory, the boulevard on the bank of the Rimac River, in the historic center of Lima, and a number of detached houses (house on Las Arenas beach and house on Pucusana Island, to the south of Lima). Currently under construction are Boulevard Miguel Dasso and a house in the north Peruvian desert.

house at las casuarinas lima peru 2005

design
Javier Artadi
structures
Meini Ingenieros S.A.C.
fixtures
Jorge Alva Machado (electrics)
Lorenzo Castro Gonzáles (sanitary)
works supervisor
Luis Noriega
client
private
location
Las Casuarinas, Lima, Peru

dimensions
1490 sqm site area
876 sqm built area

dates
2002: project
2004–05: construction

Located on the side of a hill in Las Casuarinas, the house enjoys a spectacular panorama of the city of Lima and, as a consequence of the steep slope of the ground, has one access from above and another from the park below. The residence's complex functional program comprises traditional living spaces (lounge, dining room, bedrooms) as well as special ones (gym, sauna, changing rooms, study) and a mini-apartment for guests in the upper part, while the terrace with the swimming pool faces directly onto the landscape. The design answers to the client's needs and is based on a clear-cut conceptual formulation that organizes the functional program into three "boxes," volumes which, adapting to the various levels of the plot, interpenetrate at right angles to one another in three directions: the first block contains the main vertical circulation; the sec-ond, parallel to the road, houses the bedrooms and the TV room; the third, perpendicular to the site, houses the dining room and main living room and is suspended at a height of over five meters above the ground at the front of the building which faces downhill. The remaining rooms have been located in a sort of cavity in the wall set against the ground and in two small secondary blocks. On the access level, in addition to the entrance hall and staircase, are located the garage, the laundry with its own courtyard, a spare bedroom and bathroom, a storeroom and the technical rooms. The overall image of the house is produced through a precise stereometric composition that, emphasized by the use of color and materials, creates a contrast with the natural topography of the location. In this way, the architectural object becomes an authentic belvedere onto the city.

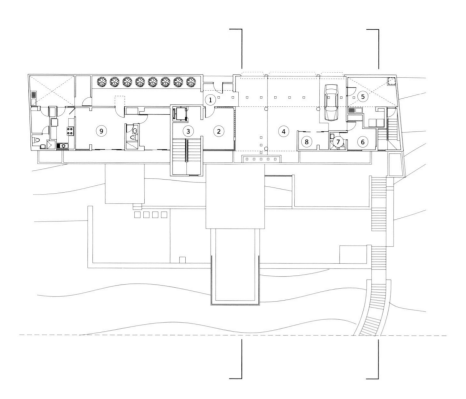

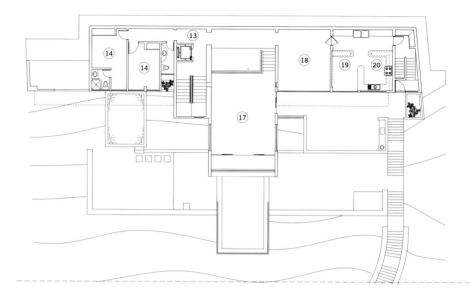

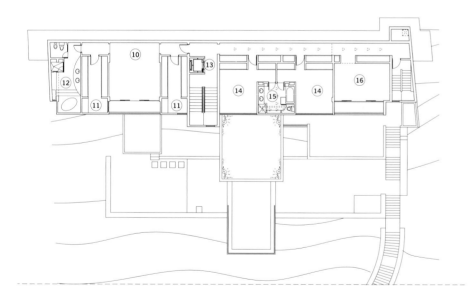

Plans of the entrance, second and third floors. Legend 1 entrance 2 entrance hall
3 hall 4 parking area 5 courtyard-laundry 6 spare bedroom 7 spare bathroom
8 storeroom-technical room 9 guests' apartment 10 double bedroom 11 wardrobe
12 master bathroom 13 entrance hall 14 bedroom 15 bathroom 16 TV room
17 main living room 18 main dining room 19 breakfast room 20 kitchen.

Main elevation and cross sections.

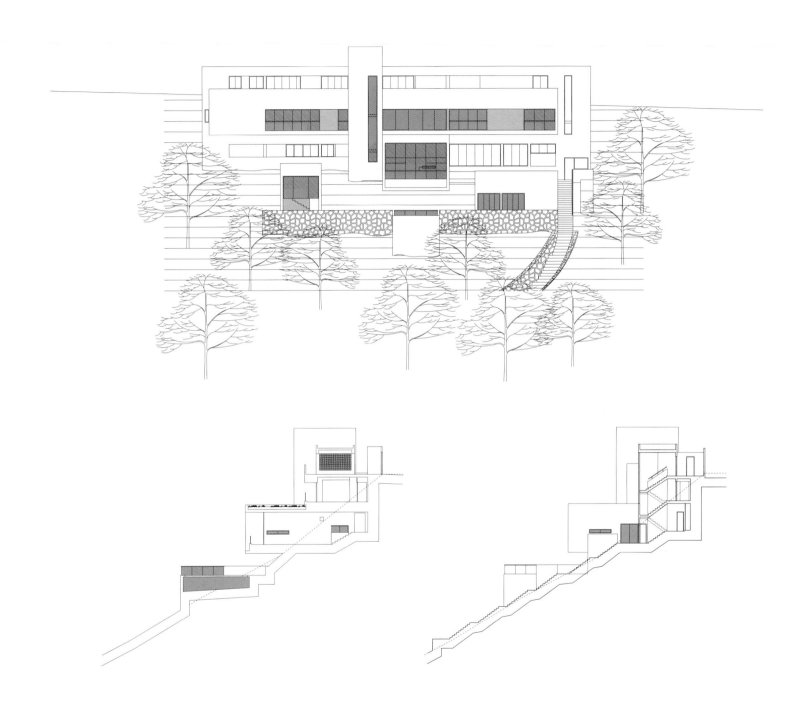

Views of the front onto the valley and the projecting volume
of the dining-living room at night.

Detail of the stairwell.

Internal views of the living room.

4 felipe assadi

Felipe Assadi (Santiago, Chile, 1971) graduated in architecture from the Finis Terrae University (UFT) in 1996. He is currently part of the program for the master's degree at the Pontifical Catholic University of Chile. In 1999 he won the "Promoción Joven" prize of the Architects Association of Chile. He teaches at the Andrés Bello University and has been a visiting professor at Talca University, Diego Portales University, the Higher Technological Institute in Monterrey, Mexico, the Autonomous University of San Luis Potosí (UASLP), Mexico, and the Bolivarian Pontifical University in Medellín, Colombia. He has lectured in several Latin American countries (Mexico, Paraguay, Venezuela) and his work has also been exhibited and published in Europe (London, Barcelona, Pamplona) and Japan. In addition to Casa Schmitz (2001), his most recent works include Casa Raveau (2004), Casa Serrano and Casa Guthrie (2005).

casa schmitz calera de tango santiago chile 2002

design
Felipe Assadi Figueroa
structure
Enzo Valladares
consultant
Guadaupe Barros, Macarena
Ugarte (landscaping)
building contractors
Constructora Moravia
client
Schmitz family
location
Lotto A2, Chacra La Primavera,
Calera de Tango, Santiago, Chile

dimensions
46,500 sqm site area
240 sqm built area

dates
2002: project and construction

Starting out from the specific conditions of the site, a fruit plantation located between the Andean Cordillera and the coastal cordillera and traversed by irrigation canals, a process of "measuring by layers" has been carried out: identification of the height of the various elements, orientation and survey of the panoramic views. To avoid altering the topography of the area excessively, the decision was taken to set the volume along the east-west axis and to adopt the grid of 4 × 4 meters derived from the orchard as a module. The analysis has led to the distinction of three functional levels. The first generates a base about one meter high, like the trunks of the fruit trees, in load-bearing masonry, whose initial section houses the technical rooms and a swimming pool. In the next segment, to the west, the base turns into a cellar, situated under the kitchen. On this double wall stands the house, like a train on tracks. The second level, coinciding with the height of the foliage, houses the day zone in a glass-walled box that projects on the two long sides of the base. Several fixed elements are visible in the design of this shell: furniture set in the façade, a concrete parallelepiped that separates the living room from the dining room and a suspended kitchen, which almost looks like a secondary unit in the common space. The third and last level is located above the crowns of the trees and houses the master bedroom. On this floor the view expands sideways to take in the two mountain ranges. Thus the opaque and introverted block on top of the building is arranged at right angles to the volumes underneath, and its openings are determined by the need to ration the amount of sunlight. Although there is a close relationship with the natural setting, the design mechanisms utilized place the accent on the purity and independence of the elements of the composition. While they may contradict the logic of the materials, they reinforce the idea of lightness: the dwelling takes on the appearance of a heavy structure of reinforced concrete supported by a fragile glass block, both of which are balanced on top of a concrete track in the middle of the countryside. A redefinition of the conventional domestic spaces has deliberately been sought, while the layout of the approach route not only negates a clear hierarchy of accesses, but also underlines the construction's character as a pavilion and therefore its condition as an object placed on the ground.

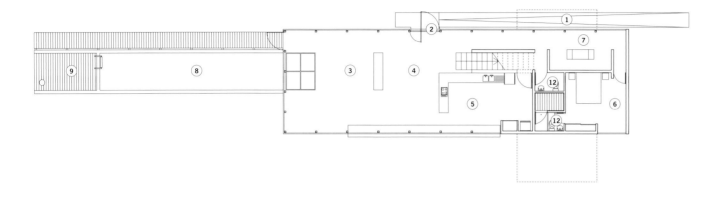

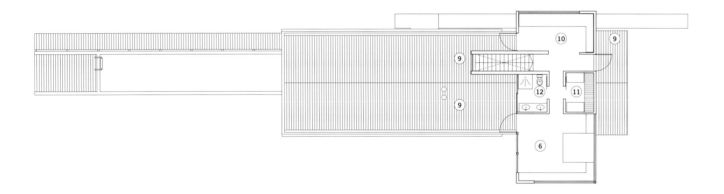

Plans of the mezzanine and second floors. Legend 1 ramp 2 entrance 3 living room
4 dining room 5 kitchen 6 bedroom 7 wardrobe 8 swimming pool 9 terrace
10 study 11 wardrobe 12 bathroom

North, south, west and east elevations.

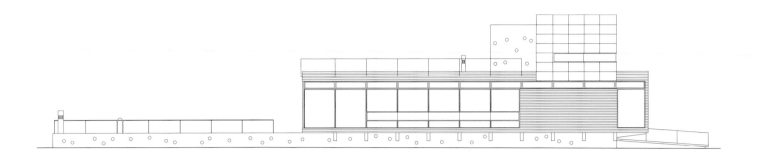

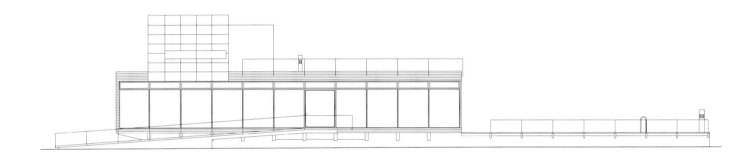

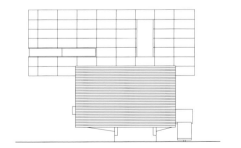

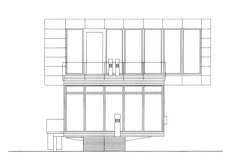

55

Views of the north and west fronts.

View from the southwest.

Views of the east front with the swimming pool and the living room at night.

The corridor.

Detail of the day zone and view of the kitchen.

5 6 barclay & crousse

Sandra Barclay (Lima, 1967) took a degree in architecture at the Ricardo Palma University in Lima in 1990 and, in 1993, a French degree in architecture at the Paris-Belleville School of Architecture (her graduation project was awarded the Robert Camelot Prize in 1994). In 2000 she was given a research grant by the Fulbright Foundation and the American Institute of Architects to study steel architecture in the United States. Jean Pierre Crousse (Lima, 1963) graduated in 1987 from the faculty of architecture of the Ricardo Palma University in Lima, where he went on to teach, an activity that he later continued at the Catholic University of Peru (1986–87). Subsequently, he took a degree in architecture from the Milan Polytechnic. In 1989 he settled in Paris, where he collaborated with the studio of Henri Ciriani until 1994. Since 1999 he has been a professor at the Paris-Belleville School of Architecture. In 1994 they founded together the Barclay & Crousse Architecture studio, concentrating their activity in France and Peru so far, and on the realization of projects characterized by an effort to achieve an integration with the natural and built landscape. Their works have received significant international recognition, including: the Record Houses Award (2004) for excellence of design; second prize for the best work constructed at the 4th Iberoamerican Biennial of Architecture (2004); first prize in the "dwellings" category at the 10th Biennial of Architecture in Peru (2002) and mentions at the "Emerging Architecture" prize (in 2001 and 2003), awarded by the magazine *The Architectural Review*. Their project for the renovation of the Musée Malraux, in addition, was selected for the Equerre d'Argent in 1999. Since 1994 they have taken part in numerous competitions, winning the ones for the renovation of the Musée Malraux (Le Havre, 1994), the conversion of a transformer of the Métro in the center of Paris into apartments (1999) and the construction of thirty-five experimental houses at Roubaix (Lille, 2004). Their recent projects include: the offices of the Valenton

houses on la escondida beach cañete peru 2001 2003

water purification plant (Paris, 2004); the renovation of the Lima Art Museum (Peru, 2004); the new Markham Theater (Peru, 2005). Among the works constructed: the racetrack at Rambouillet (France, 2005); ninety-six apartments in Montreuil (Paris, 2005); the renovation of the town hall of Epinay-sur-Seine (France, 2004); the offices of Le Gambetta at Malakoff (Paris, 2003); the Musée Malraux (Le Havre, 1999); three houses on the Peruvian desert coast (1999–2003) and, finally, a house in the countryside near Toulouse (France, 2005). Their works have been published in numerous specialist magazines and shown at exhibitions in Lima (2004), London (2003), Santiago in Chile (2003), Copenhagen (2001), Le Havre (2000) and Paris (1996 and 1997).

The two designs attempt to "tame" the uncompromising nature of one of the driest deserts in the world, on the Pacific coast, without betraying or negating it and seeking the intimacy necessary to inhabit such a location through integration of the dwelling into a territory highly sensitive to objects that alter its equilibrium. The result, therefore, of a reflection on the dichotomy between closure and opening, opacity and brightness, tradition and modernity, Casa M (2001) echoes on the outside some of the characteristics of the buildings constructed on the ocean shore. Thus an elementary and introverted disposition of masses determines an abstract composition that establishes a relationship with the surrounding landscape, while the creation of an enclosure protects the domestic space. Inside, boundaries disappear to multiply the intersecting views of the outside, characterized by the use of light and the continual search for transparence. The functional division into three blocks permits the development of a sequence of spaces that, following the slope of the ground, leads from the patio of access to the double-height gallery of the living room, culminating in the terrace with the swimming pool overlooking the sea. In the case of Casa X, a twofold strategy of design has been pursued to attain the same objectives: the maximum occupation of the space suitable for building and the definition of a solid block and not of a simple volumetric boundary. Out of this has come a pure prism, "stranded" on the dunes, which seems as if its been there forever. This "preexistent" solid has subsequently been hollowed out, extracting material to create and simultaneously reveal the various rooms. This logic of "ablation" (removal), antithetical to the additive system typical of construction, defines areas delimited by a built perimeter, inside which the ambiguity between closed and open spaces is considerably heightened. Here too access to the enclosure is through a threshold that unites and separates two external spaces: the boundless one of the desert and the more intimate one of the entrance patio. The patio is extended toward the ocean by means of a terrace conceived as an artificial beach, culminating in a long and narrow swimming pool that forms a link with the sea and the horizon. The roof, a large horizontal plane that spans the entire width of the lot, frames the seascape and protects the living room like a parasol. The boundary between this room and the solarium is broken down by a sliding door of tempered glass. A flight of steps, running parallel to the slope of the ground, connects the entrance level to that of the bedrooms below. Along the lateral extension of the intermediate landing are ranged the children's and guests' bedrooms, screened by the wooden deck of the upper terrace. At the end of the staircase, the swimming pool acts as a roof to a balconied gallery facing onto the sea, providing access to the bedroom of the owners of the house. The ocher color, frequently utilized in pre-Columbian and Hispanic constructions on the Peruvian coast, avoids the aging in the appearance of the buildings as a result of sandstorms.

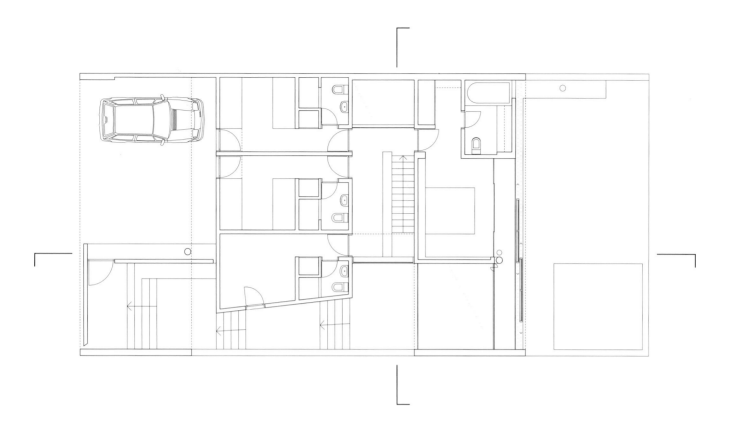

Casa M 2001

design
Sandra Barclay,
Jean Pierre Crousse
structure
Carlos Casabone
works supervisor
Edward Barclay
building contractors
Centec SA
client
private
location
La Escondida beach,
Cañete province, Peru

dimensions
253 sqm site area
156 sqm built area

dates
2000: project
2001: construction

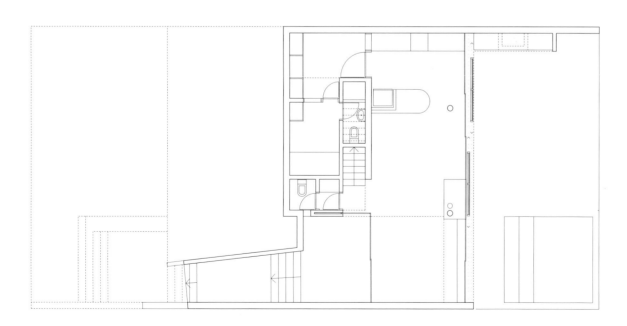

Plans of the access floor and basement.

North elevation, longitudinal section and cross section of the stairwell.

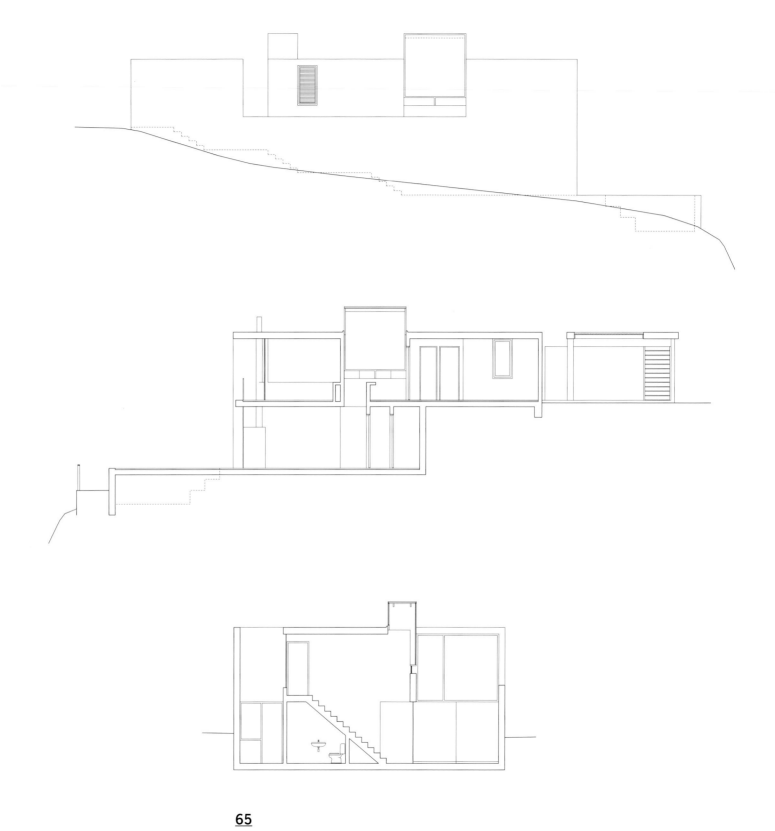

65

Views of the two houses from the sea and the cliff.

External view of the northwest corner.

North front and entrance patio.

The loggia facing the Pacific Ocean from the entrance patio and entrance staircase.

The loggia seen from the swimming pool and internal view the living room opening onto the terrace.

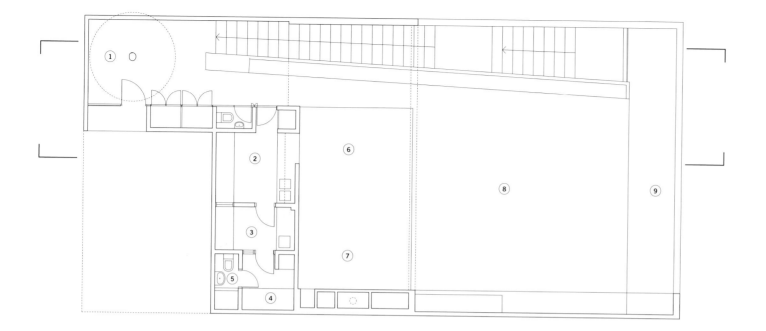

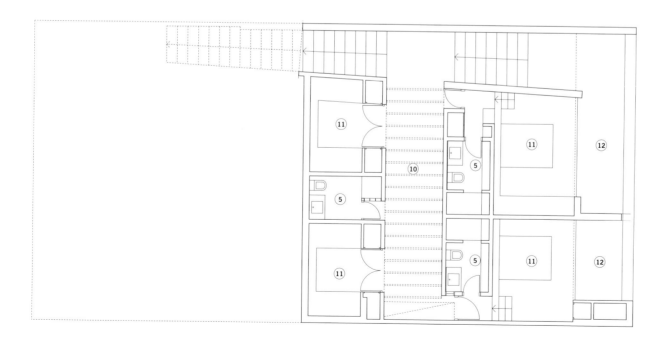

Casa X 2003

design
Sandra Barclay,
Jean Pierre Crousse
structure
Llanos & Flores S.A.
works supervisor
Edward Barclay
building contractors
Constructora Edward Barclay
client
private
location
La Escondida beach, Cañete
province, Peru

dimensions
253 sqm site area
174 sqm built area

dates
2002: project
2003: construction

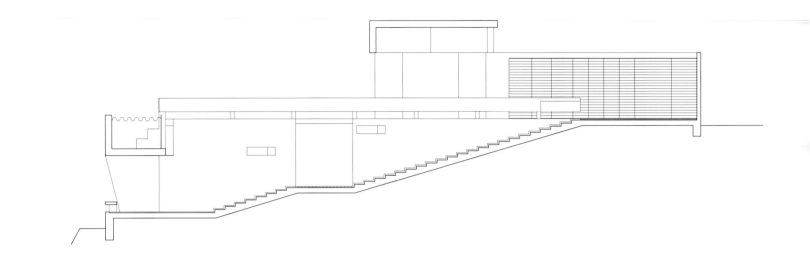

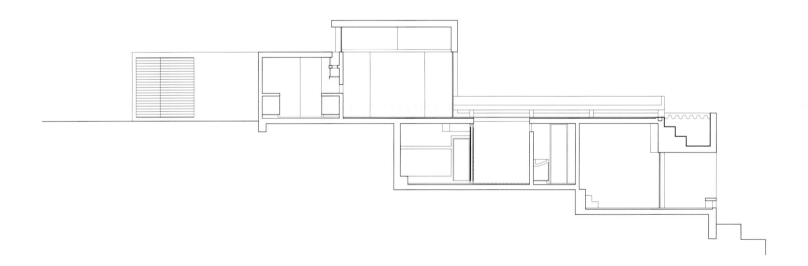

Plans of the ground floor and basement. Legend 1 entrance 2 kitchen 3 patio
4 spare bedroom 5 bathroom 6 dining room 7 living room 8 terrace
9 swimming pool 10 corridor 11 bedroom 12 balcony.

Longitudinal section on the external and central staircase.

The balcony of the master bedroom.

Views of the external staircase from above and below.

The parapet-seat of the solarium.

Views of the terrace with the swimming pool and of the entrance.

The terrace overlooking the sea viewed from the adjacent house and the corridor of the bedrooms.

The entrance patio.

Corner of the suspended swimming pool.

View looking toward the sea from the entrance and detail of the balcony of the double bedroom.

Views of the terrace, with the open-air dining area, and of the living room screened by the awning made of aluminum and permeable elastic fabric.

7

clusellas & colle

Mariano Clusellas (Buenos Aires, 1963) graduated in 1989 from the Faculty of Architecture, Design and City Planning of the University of Buenos Aires—where he has also held the teaching posts of Horacio Baliero and Justo Solsona—and has been a visiting professor at Palermo University, the Center de Estudios de Arquitectura Contemporánea of the Torcuato Di Tella University (CEAC / UTDT) in Buenos Aires and at the Pontifical Catholic University in Santiago, Chile. He has also given lectures and taken part in group exhibitions in Argentina (Museo de Bellas Artes in Buenos Aires) and abroad (PUC in Santiago, Chile, Houston Fine Arts Museum, Iberoamerican Institute in Berlin). In collaboration with various professional studios he has participated in numerous competitions (new headquarters of the CELS, headquarters of the J.L. Borges Foundation, Pepsi Cola offices, renovation of Porto Madero). His more significant works include: the yellow house (1995–2000, with H. Baliero and C. Alvis), the house on the precipice (1997, with H. Baliero), the

Casas de la Rambla Building (2000) and the water tower on the river (2000), all in Colonia del Sacramento; the project for a detached house at Piriápolis (1999, with G. Cabrera), Casa Camorino (2000) and the Dabbah & Torrejón art gallery (2000) in Buenos Aires; the country house at San Pedro and the second house on the precipice, both in Colonia (2001). Among his most recent detached houses, those of Pilar, Ezeiza and Tigre (2005). Sebastián Colle (Buenos Aires, 1973) graduated in 2003 from the Faculty of Architecture, Design and City Planning of the University of Buenos Aires, where he has also carried out academic activities (1999–2004). He has contributed to specialist magazines and taken part in numerous competitions. Among the projects he has realized with Mariano Clusellas, it is worth mentioning Casa Casaretto, in Buenos Aires, and Casa Ichaso at La Horqueta (2005); currently under construction two detached houses (in Buenos Aires and Santa Barbara) and the Washington Building at Coghlan, Argentina.

house at josé ignacio uruguay 2005

design
Mariano Clusellas
Sebastián Colle
collaborators
Cristian O'Connor, Alberto
Campolonghi, Rodolfo Crocce,
Juan Ades
structure
Helio Pazos
consultants
Rosa Oks, Marta Weil
(landscaping)
building contractors
Rubén Martínez, Constructora
General
fixtures
Rubén Urrutia (electrics)
Luis de León (sanitary)
Heber Torres (doors and windows)
client
private
location
José Ignacio, Uruguay

dimensions
6500 sqm site area
1340 sqm built area

dates
2003: project
2004–05: construction

The house is situated in the vicinity of a fishing village located near a lighthouse, on a small peninsula on the Atlantic coast. The lot is characterized by a steep slope and is surrounded by country paths and the beach. The position of the building offers a sweeping view of the bay, to the northeast, and of the lighthouse and village, to the southeast. Two different and contrasting scales coexist in the project, structured through courtyards and passages. The roof slopes in the opposite direction to the ground, in order to control the proportions of the entrance courtyard and increase the height of the fronts facing onto the sea. Thus the roofs are tilted toward the entrance and the large stone walls face toward the beach. Entering from the highest point, the horizon is visible. Below extends the surface of tiles, whose color blends with the sand. The entrance patio is comprised between the two side wings and two inclined retaining walls. As the site is very windy and lacks natural barriers, the courtyard serves as a shelter, protected to the southeast by the house and exposed, to the west, to the afternoon sun. From here it is possible to view the sea through several gaps and special windows. In addition to clearly delimited open spaces, with a controlled height and domestic character, it houses the swimming pool, several steps lower down. On the upper floor, level with the courtyard, the house turns into a large gallery-balcony, where the main living areas are located. Between walls, roofs and eaves, openings of various sizes frame distant views. In the connection between the two wings is set a terrace overlooking the sea, which doubles up the indoor living functions thanks to its covering with a wooden lattice that, in a similar way to the one over the open-air dining room, filters the midday light. The lower floor, sunk slightly into the ground, houses small rooms—bedrooms, toilets and other spaces, determining the various changes in level of the floor above. The building is constructed with traditional, craft methods, using natural materials: wood, granite and local limestone. The irregular surfaces and joints, together with the marked textures, accentuate the rustic character of the house.

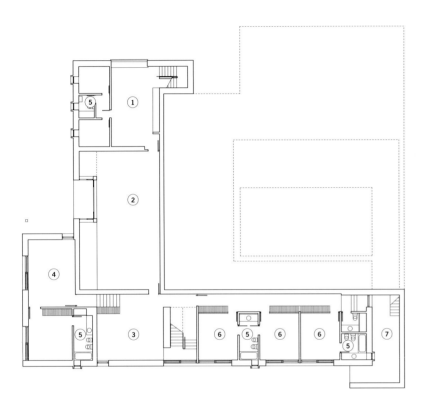

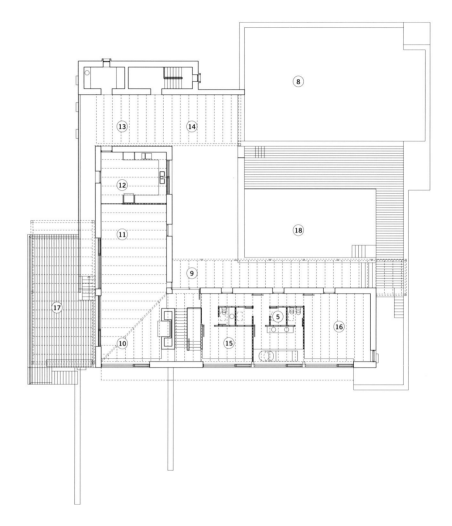

Plans of the ground and second floors. Legend 1 garage and services
2 games room 3 TV room 4 guests' bedrooms 5 bathroom 6 bedrooms 7 patio
8 entrance patio 9 entrance 10 living room 11 dining room 12 kitchen
13 open-air dining area 14 pergola 15 studio 16 double bedroom 17 terrace
18 swimming pool.

West, south and east elevations.

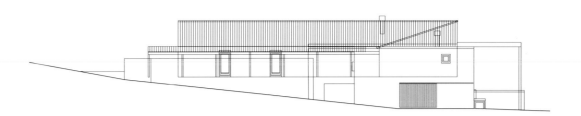

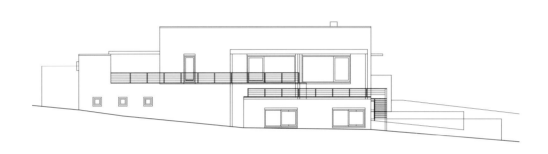

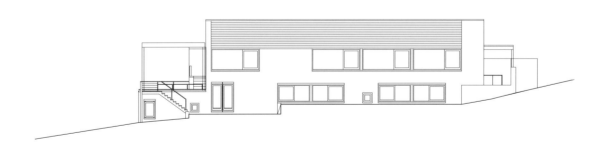

87

Views from the south and east.

View of the east front.

Detail of the eastern façade and the patio of the swimming pool viewed from the north.

Details of the terrace to the south, the courtyard and entrance zone, all screened by wooden pergolas.

Internal views of the living and TV rooms.

The stairwell.

8

ga grupo arquitectura / daniel alvarez

Daniel Alvarez (Mexico City, 1960) graduated in 1981 from the Iberoamerican University, where he now teaches. Since then, he has practiced the profession in association with other architects under the name Grupo Arquitectura. Until 1997, he worked in partnership with Alberto Kalach. He has won numerous competitions and shown his work at exhibitions in Mexico and abroad. Visiting professor at various universities in Mexico and the United States, he is currently collaborating on housing programs, taking responsibility for the design, the planning and the property development. Among the projects he has realized, numerous detached houses (Lomas de Chapultepaec, 2003; Cuernavaca and Tepoztlán, Morelos, 2004; Bosques de Santa Fe, Bosques de las Lomas, 2005), residential buildings (at Holbein 67, 1991; Flores Magón 130, 1993; Prieto 1643, 1994; Lamartine 125, 2003; Ocampo 463, 2003; Amsterdam 226, Musset 310, Caldern de la Barca 86, Rio de La Plata 28, Mexicali 15, Sullivan 49, 2004), and offices (at Observatorio 444, 1993; Alica 46, Mexico D.F. 2003), all in Mexico City. Several apartment buildings have just been completed in Puerto Peñasco, San Miguel Chapultepec, Mexico City, Guadalajara and Acapulco.

casa izar valle de bravo mexico 2002

design
GA Grupo Arquitectura
Daniel Alvarez
LVF & Asociados
collaborators
Raúl Chavez, Rosa López,
Susana López, Alfonso Magaña,
Victoria Montoya, Rafael Navarro,
Andrei Olivares, Vanessa Padilla,
Petra Quiroz, Rafael Sánchez,
Julieta Toral, Sergio Valdés,
Lorena Vieyra
structure
Enrique Camarena Labadie
building contractors
GA Grupo Arquitectura
Daniel Alvarez
client
private
location
Valle de Bravo, Mexico

dimensions
3600 sqm site area
700 sqm built area

dates
2001: project
2002: construction

The house is located near a slope and extends with accentuated horizontality in the middle of a conifer wood. The slender parallel lines that define the disposition of masses take on concrete form in the two guiding elements of the composition—floor and roof—and configure a continuous strip that rests directly on the ground at one end, but is suspended in the air for the rest of its length in an attempt to break free of the irregular terrain. The pronounced slope has led to the use of a metal structure to raise the greater part of the building above ground. The structure forms a sort of porch stretching for 40 meters, which supports a sloping roof independent of the partition walls. Its inverted ridge imparts a soaring line to the front view and orients the vistas. The tapering of the roof augments the view of the landscape from the inside and avoids the roof entering into contact with the partitions, which organize the functional program with their discreet presence. To enter the house you pass through a courtyard ringed with stone walls and then along the edge of a long and narrow pool of water that leads to the outer threshold, made of travertine. Beyond the service block, located to the left of the entrance, the day zone occupies the northern corner of the plan, with a large terrace that runs around the perimeter, linking up with the bedrooms. The presence of water accentuates the material dissolution of the architectural object through a dialogue between the built and the natural context that is capable of softening the outlines and concealing their metal structure in the dense vegetation of the surroundings.

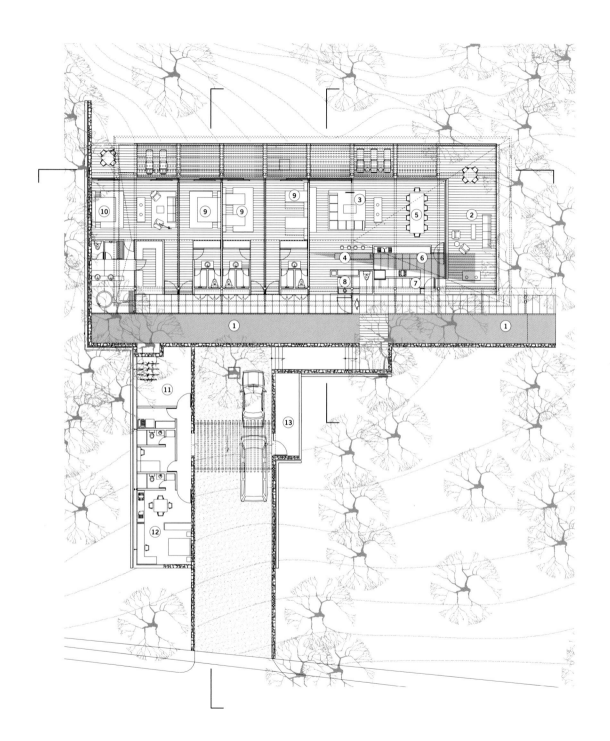

Plan. Legend 1 pool 2 terrace 3 living room 4 bar 5 dining room 6 kitchen 7 larder 8 toilets 9 bedroom 10 double bedroom 11 cellar 12 services 13 technical room.

Cross and longitudinal sections.

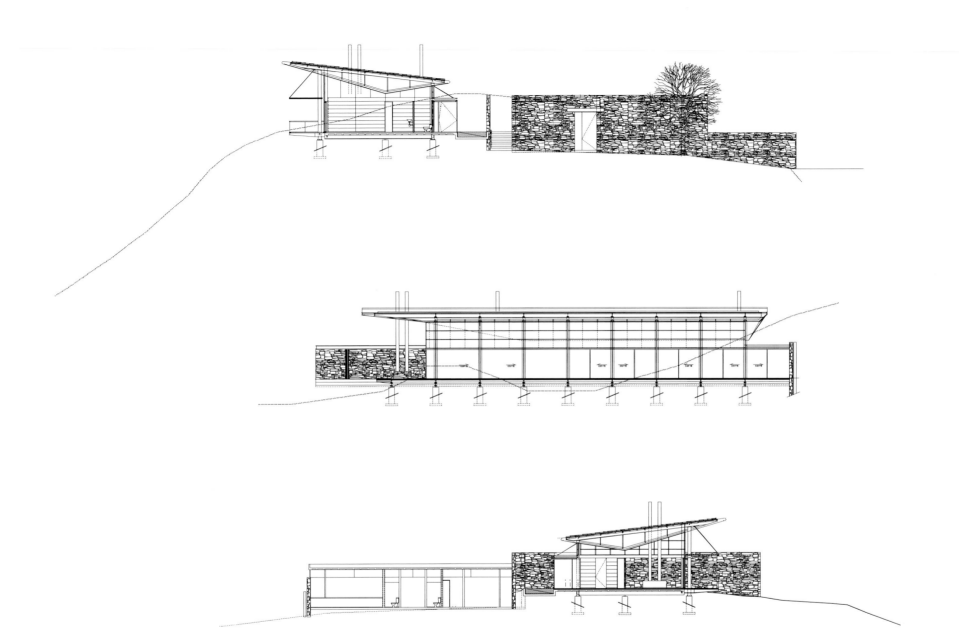

Views of the house from the wood.

Views of the external terrace and of the house from the wood at night and detail of the pond.

Views of the open-air living area on the terrace next to the dining zone.

9 alberto kalach

Alberto Kalach (Mexico City, 1960) graduated in architecture from the Iberoamerican University of Mexico, in 1981, and from Cornell University, Ithaca, New York, in 1985. He has taught at Houston University, the University of Southern California, Harvard University Graduate School of Design and the Polytechnic University of Puerto Rico. He currently holds the "Ciudad de México" chair at the UNAM (Autonomous University of Mexico). He has had exhibitions and given lectures at various academic institutions in Mexico and abroad (Puerto Rico, United States, Spain and France). Over the course of his career he has participated in numerous national and international competitions, with projects of architecture and city planning on every scale (from minimal housing to the scheme for the environmental rehabilitation of the catchment basin of Mexico City). Along with Casa Negro, his more significant works include: the detached house in Valle di Bravo (1993); Casa Palmira at Cuernavaca (Morelos, 1994); Casa GGG (1999) and Casa Mojada (2003), both in Mexico City; La Atalaya House in California (2003–05); Casa de Cima, Contadero (2005); and Casa Bross at Lomas de Santa Fe (2005). Again in the Mexican capital: the Adolf (1996), Balderas (1996) and Parroquia buildings (1999). Among his recent projects: the Augen research center at Ensenada (Baja California, 2000); the Atalaya del Mar housing complex in California (2000); the Sombrerete building, Condesa (2003); the Buenavista station (2005); a high school in Guadalajara (2005); and five different branches of the new technological school (Coacalco, Ixtapaluca, Cuautitlán, Tecamac and Aragón, 2005). Currently under construction, the El Faro arts and crafts workshops at Istapalapa; the Casa en el agua at Nanjing, China; the hospital of Parral, Chihuahua; the Monte Sinaí temple; and the José Vasconcelos Library of Mexican Library, Mexico City.

casa negro contadero mexico 1997

design
Alberto Kalach
with Daniel Alvarez
collaborators
Rosa López,
Gustavo Lipkau
structure
Guillermo Tena
building contractors
Constructora Desp
works supervisor
Daniel Alvarez
Fernández
consultants
Jorge Segura
(blacksmith),
Tonatiuth Martínez
(garden)
client
private
location
Contadero, Mexico

dimensions
2000 sqm site area
700 sqm built area

dates
1995: project
1997: construction

Starting out from a thorough analysis of the site's morphology, the five blocks that make up the house rest, like floating platforms, on a steep wooded slope. Three of these architectural elements are located on paths where there are no trees, in an attempt to alter the site as little as possible, while guaranteeing the living spaces a magnificent panoramic view. In keeping with this approach, the supports of the bridges have been kept to a minimum, in order to avoid the construction of retaining walls that would have altered the contour of the ground. In addition, the foundations generate a set of cisterns that store the rainwater running off terraces and courtyards. In this way the design organizes the spaces of the house while respecting the topography and vegetation and seeking the most suitable orientations. The functional program defines the proportions and the materials of the different blocks, which house respectively the kitchen with its services, the entrance with the living room and dining room, the bedrooms, the study and the swimming pool. The use of lightly colored concrete for the walls, the façades of marble, steel and glass and the floors of stone, wood or "water" emphasize the effort to create contrasts, gradations, textures and reflections that establish a dynamic relationship with the landscape. The geometric clarity of the layout does not impede the spatial articulation of the various rooms, with the interstices generated by inflections of the volumes. In this way a fluid ambiguity between inside and outside is created which helps to establish a continuity between the built and the natural. This house, which has been "sown like a tree" whose roots, trunk and branches have adapted progressively to the ground as they grow, has blended completely into the wood, becoming part of it. In the design an attempt has been made to establish an immediate and lasting relationship between the building and its environmental context: "The house has been cultivated in the manner one cultivates a garden," observes Kalach, "and, as such, remains in a state of constant transformation."

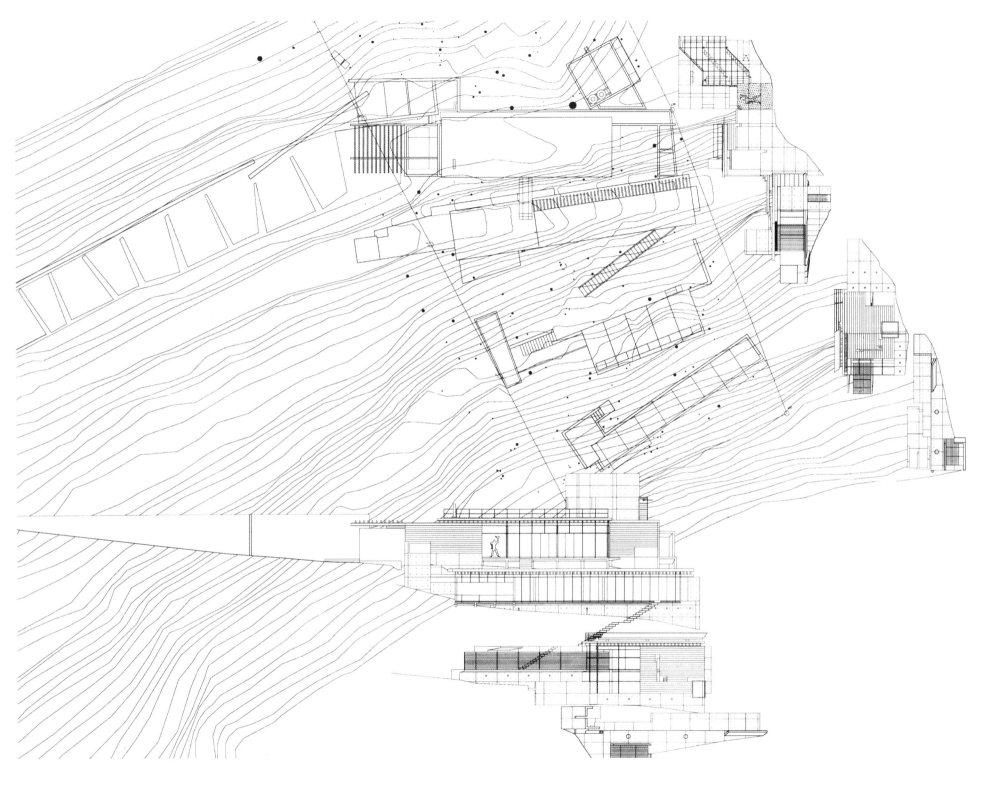

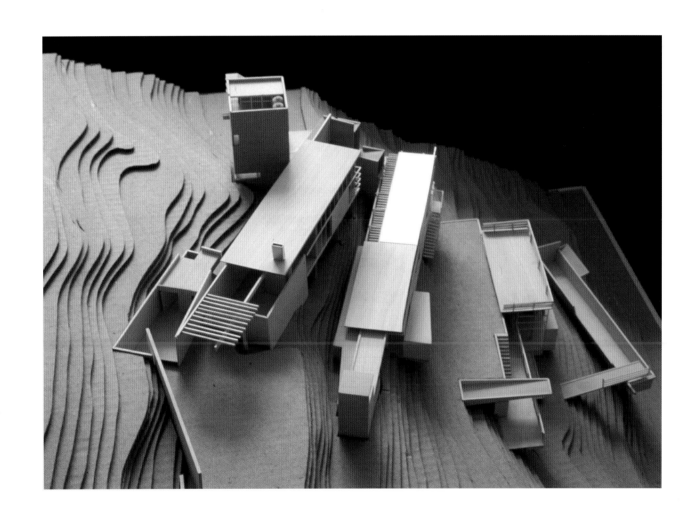

Site plan, sections and elevations.

View of the study model.

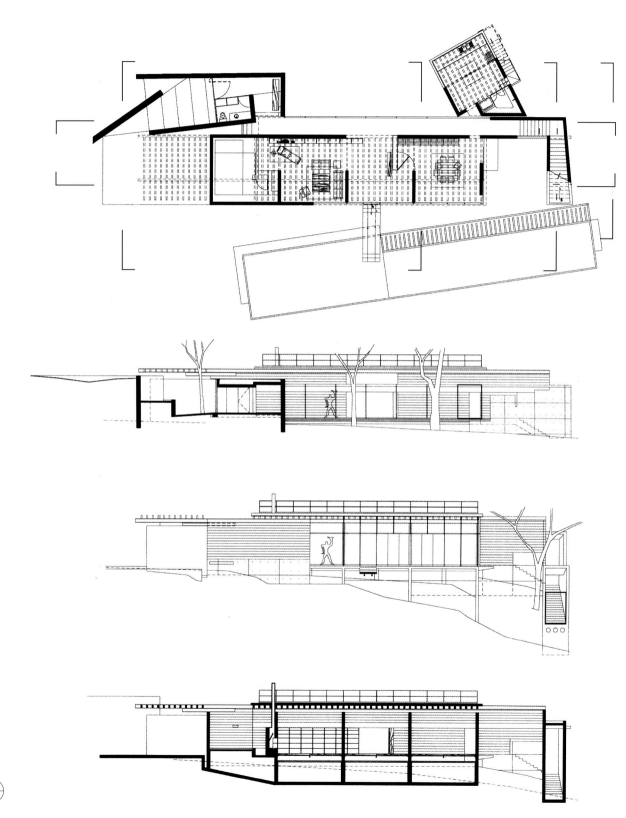
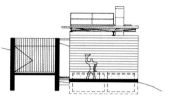

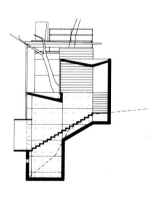

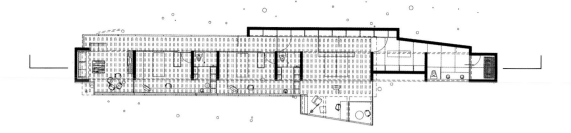

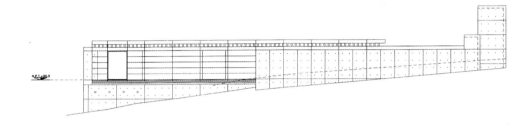

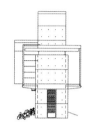

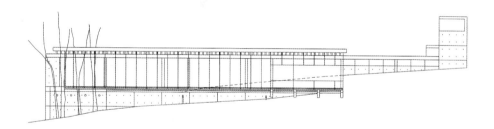

Plan, sections and elevations of the day zone.

Plan, sections and elevations of the volume
housing the bedrooms.

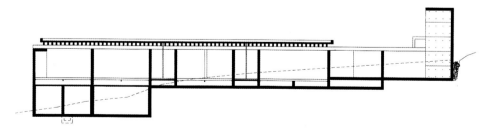

The block of the living room is reflected in the glazed section and the surface of the water on the roof of the night zone.

View of the house in the wood from the southeast.
View of the upper entrance to the pavilion of the studio.

The pool of water on the roof of the block of bedrooms.

The entrance at the lower level of the studio.

The east end of the day zone and the tower of the kitchen and utility rooms. Detail of the patio providing access to the living room.

Details of the two ends of the day zone.

Internal views of the day zone, open space subdivided by raw cc

10

mathias klotz

Mathias Klotz Germain (Viña del Mar, 1965) graduated from the Pontifical Catholic University of Chile in 1991, where he taught from 1997 to 1999. He has also taught at the Federico Santa Maria University in Valparaíso (1996–2000), the Central University of Santiago (1996–98) and the Department of Architecture, Art and Design of the Diego Portales University (2001–05), of which he has been principal since 2001. He has published his projects and articles in numerous international architecture journals and held lectures and seminars abroad, where he has often exhibited his work. With Casa Müller he won the "Under 40" prize of the Architects Association of Chile in 1995, while Casa Klotz was selected by the International Union of Architects in 1996. A finalist for the Mies van der Rohe Award in 1998 and 2000, he has received mentions at the Santiago Biennial of Architecture, the Miami Biennial (2002) and the Borromini Prize (2001). Since Casa Klotz, built at Playa Grande de Tongoy (1991), and the better-known Casa Müller on Chiloé Island (1993), he has constructed a large number of detached houses. Among his more recent works it is worth mentioning: the Safex Building in the Valle de Llay Llay (1996); the head offices of Pizarras Ibéricas at Huechuraba (1997); the Entel Pavilion in Santiago (1998) the Las Niñas Cellar in Santa Cruz (1999–2000); the Altamira College in Santiago (1999–2000); the Smol Shopping Center at Concepción (2002); the military shelters at Farellonea (2002); and the Departments of Medicine (2003–04) and Economics (2005–) of the Diego Portales University in Santiago. Currently under construction are a house for the CIPEA (China International Practical Exhibition of Architecture) in Nanjing; Casa Ladybrook at Mijas, Spain; Casa Techos at Villa Angostura, Argentina; two houses at Punta del Este, Uruguay; Atassi House at Faqra and the Ozone Building in Beirut, Lebanon; Casa de la Cuadra a Santo Domingo, Dominican Republic; and, in Chile again, Casa Kegevic at Zapallar, Casa Diaz at Aculeo and Casa Lo Curro and the Bernstein and Klotz house-studio in Santiago.

casa ponce san isidro buenos aires argentina 2003

design
Mathias Klotz
collaborator
Pablo Riquelme
landscaping
Juan Grimm
structure
Enzo Valladares
building contractors
Stieglitz
client
Hernán Ponce
location
Perdriel 1540, San Isidro, Buenos
Aires, Argentina

dimensions
2000 sqm site area
570 sqm built area

dates
2000: project
2001–03: construction

The house stands in a well-known residential district of Buenos Aires dating from the forties, on an extremely long, narrow and steeply sloping site, surrounded by dense vegetation. The topographical conformation of the site—a ravine facing onto the bank of the Rio de La Plata—means that anyone living there can enjoy a magnificent panorama. For this reason, the objective of Mathias Klotz's design has been to leave the wonderful view of the river free, in such a way that the house does not interrupt the spatial continuity between the front and rear portions of the plot. This has led to the creation of a fluid and dynamic pathway, outlined by the entrance footbridge, that accentuates this programmatic and spatial principle in an elegant manner. Functional requirements determined the construction of two blocks floating above a basement. The access level, occupied by spaces for common use, the kitchen, several terraces and the swimming pool, is characterized by a parallelepiped with glass walls that establishes a visual connection with the surroundings in all directions. The upper floor, where the bedrooms are located, is housed in a more enclosed block, linked directly with the roof terrace. On the lower floor, in addition to the technical plant, are located the service rooms: laundry, cellar and a second bedroom. Thus the house is composed of a series of strong contrasts, from the viewpoint of both its disposition of masses and its structure, with the solid slab of the night zone set on top of a light and transparent volume, which in turn rests on a base sunk into the ground. A balanced dynamics of composition emphasizes the contrasting character of the architectural elements.

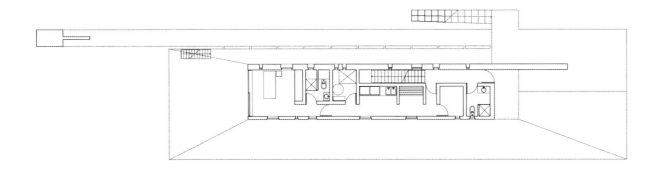

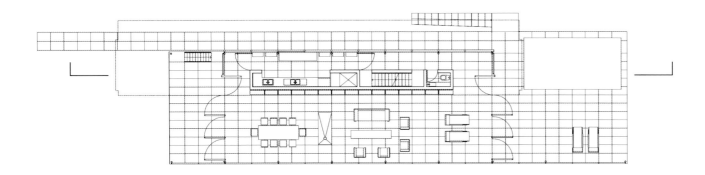

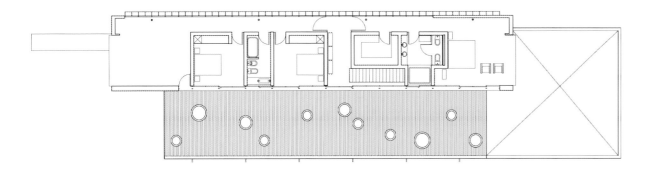

Plans of the basement and the ground and second floors.

North elevation, longitudinal section through the stairs and west and east elevations.

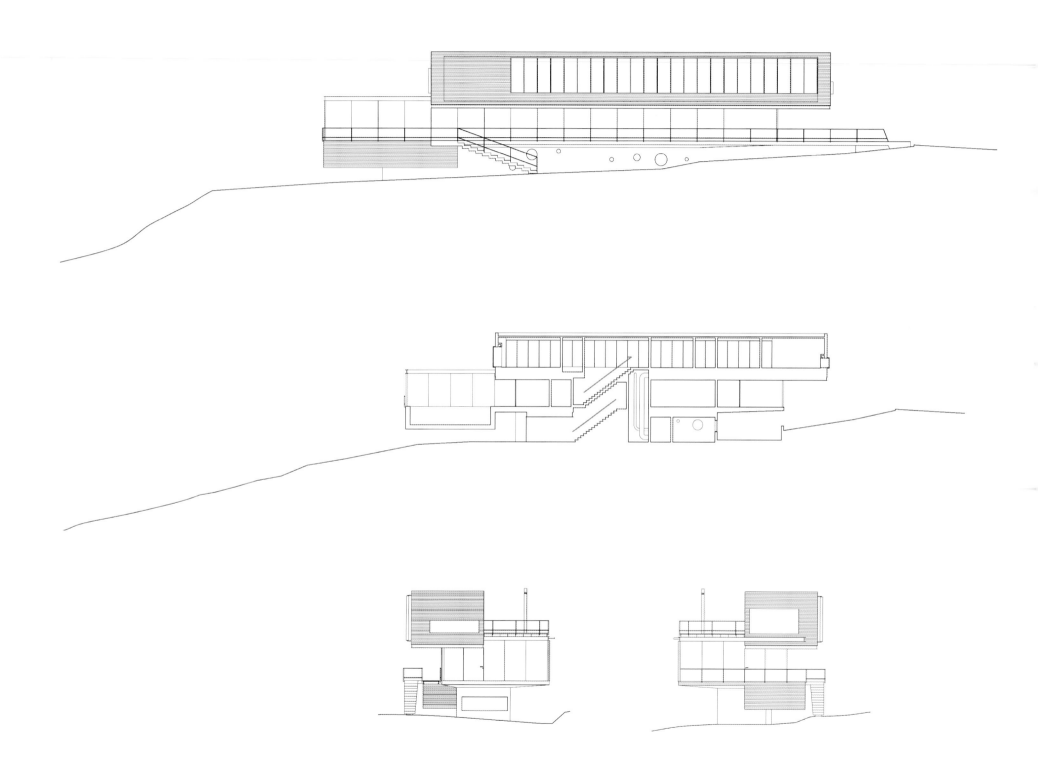

Views of the east and west front.

Views of the west front from the access walkway and from the terrace with the swimming pool at the other end, facing onto the Rio de La Plata.

The terrace of the bedrooms on the second floor.

Views of the swimming pool terrace from the balcony on the second floor and from the living room.

The dining room behind the block of the fireplace.

Views of the walkway along the north front and the corridor of the bedrooms.

11 marcio kogan

Marcio Kogan (São Paulo, 1952) graduated from the Faculty of Architecture of Mackenzie University in 1976. His work has received wide recognition in the field of design as well as architecture (Barilla Prize in 1992; 4th São Paulo Biennial of Architecture in 1999; finalist for the World Architecture Award in 2002; mention at the 4th Iberoamerican Biennial and Record Houses in 2004). He has taken part in various group exhibitions ("Ornithological Architecture," 1998; "Architecture and Humor," 1995 and 2001, both at the MBC in São Paulo; "Happyland" at the 25th São Paulo Biennial of Art, 2002; "Involucri," Bologna, 2002 and "Encore Moderne? Architecture brésilienne 1928–2005," Paris, 2005). He practices in occasional partnership with Isay Weinfeld, with whom he designed, Casa Goldfarb (1991), among others. His competition projects include the one for the new Puc-Campinas church (2001); the Museum of Microbiology and the Cultural Center of the "Corpo" dance group in São Paulo (2002). He is a member of the Instituto dos Arquitetos do Brasil (AAB) and of the Associação Brasileria dos Escritórios de Arquitetura (AsBEA). Among the works constructed, in addition to Casa du Plessis, Casa Gama Issa at Alto de Pinheiros (2001), Casa Quinta in São Paulo (2004) and Casa BR at Araras, Rio de Janeiro (2004).

casa du plessis paraty brazil 2003

design
Marcio Kogan
with Diana Radomysler
and Cassia Cavani
collaborators
Bruno Gomes, Oswaldo Pessano,
Regiane Leão, Renata Furlanetto,
Samanta Cafardo,
Suzana Glogowski
structure
Fernando Vasconcelos
Alberto Du Plessis
Francisco Vasconcellos
Gramont Engenharia
building contractors
Dp Unique
consultants
Marcelo Faisal (landscaping)
clients
Patricia and Alberto Du Plessis
location
Paraty, Rio de Janeiro, Brazil

dimensions
990 sqm site area
406 sqm built area

dates
2001: project
2003: construction

The house is located in the Laranjeiras condominium, a few kilometers from the historic city of Paraty, a tourist attraction for the inhabitants of São Paulo and Rio de Janeiro owing to the beauty of its jagged coastline and its proximity to the forest. The search for an architectural solution that would be modern and traditional at one and the same time has led to the adoption of an essential disposition of masses. This has made it possible to come up with a fully contemporary design from the expressive viewpoint, while complying with the building regulations that require the use of terracotta roofing tiles. The functional program is organized around a rectangular patio that serves as the entrance: on the longest side are ranged four bedrooms with their respective bathrooms and the TV room, facing onto the courtyard with wooden lattices that filter the light, while the day zone (lounge, terrace and swimming pool) is concentrated at the more sheltered back of the plot. A trellis of bamboo, hung underneath movable transparent panels, permits adaptation of the room to changes in the weather. A band of utility rooms (kitchen, larder, bedroom with bathroom) with a separate entrance concludes the plan to the north. The box, clad with stone from Minas Gerais and hollowed out by the courtyard, contains a row of four jaboticaba trees (*Myrciaria cauliflora*) in the middle of the paving of cobblestones as a tamed presence of the forest. The continual overlap between open and closed spaces, conceived to bring the most significant elements of the surroundings—light, vegetation, air—into the house, in combination with the sensitivity shown in the choice and use of local materials, creates atmospheres of particular refinement.

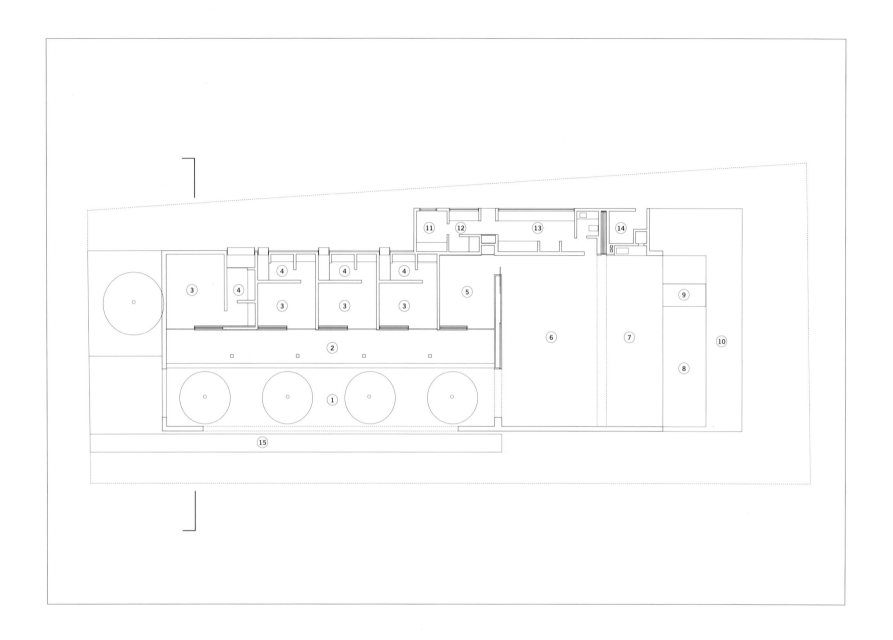

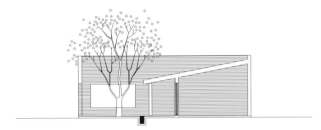

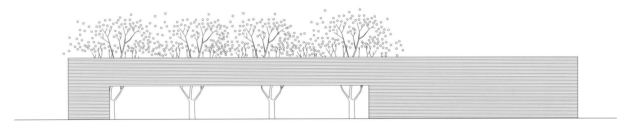

Plan. Legend 1 patio 2 corridor 3 bedroom 4 bathroom 5 TV room 6 living room
7 terrace 8 swimming pool 9 wooden bridge 10 solarium 11 spare bedroom
12 laundry 13 kitchen 14 storeroom 15 entrance deck.

South elevation and cross section.

Views of the southeast front and patio.

Details of the front onto the road and the porch on the patio.

View of the patio from west.

The system of screens of the bedrooms.

Internal view of the living room adjacent to the swimming pool.

12

leopoldo laguinge

Leopoldo Laguinge (Córdoba, Argentina 1955) graduated in architecture from the Catholic University of Córdoba in 1979 and took a master's degree at the University of Cincinnati (OH), in 1985. He carries out teaching and research activities at these institutions, along with the National and Pascal University of Córdoba, Argentina, and Washington University, St. Louis (MO). He commenced his professional practice in the United States as a collaborator of the Skidmore, Owings & Merrill firm in Chicago (1985–86) and Bohm NBBJ in Columbus (1986–88), going on to work for the Argentinean branch of Delta Constructions Industries (1990) and the B. Roggio Empresa Constructora (1990), while setting up the Larqs studio in 1991. In addition to several detached houses (1991–2000) in the city of Córdoba, it is worth mentioning the FR92 apartment building (1992), the Museum of Religious Art of the San José Monastery (1994), the renovation of the auditorium of the university's Language School (1996), the offices (administration, canteen and services) of Aguas Cordobesas (1999–2000) and the plans for two residential districts (2001). Among his more recent projects near of Córdoba, the house on the waterfall (2005) and the house among the trees (2005), and Casa Laguinge (2002–06).

detached house at quintas de san antonio córdoba argentina 1998

design
Leopoldo Laguinge
structure
Huerta, Pratto & Payer
consultants
Fabio Roda (heating system)
client
Elena Garlot
location
Quintas de San Antonio, Córdoba,
Argentina

dimensions
6100 sqm site area
290 sqm built area

dates
1997: project
1998: construction

Located in the environs of the city of Córdoba, this country house is defined by the geometric pattern of the cultivated fields in whose midst it is constructed: rectangular plots of land surrounded by poplars or evergreen trees that line the irrigation channels and follow the endless undulations that mechanically model the quiet landscape of furrowed surfaces. It is in this rural fabric that the dwelling takes shape, inside a rectangular enclosure (110 × 55 meters) formed of *pircacóna*—the characteristic dry-stone walls of the region—and covered with a suspended roof. Abstraction is the stratagem of design chosen as a response to the immense expanse of surrounding land, where the certainty of the masses of stone, the heavy sliding wooden shutters and the linearity of the thick roof beams of reinforced concrete act as an "anchoring" to the ground for a building that has to contend with the continuity of the horizon. The tower of the water tanks forms a compositional counterpoint and rises vertically in the attempt to create a landmark. Inside, like a tangible refuge from the vertigo of an uncontrollable scale, several "white boxes" alternating with courtyards house the various domestic activities, establishing relations of permeability with the outside and interacting dynamically with one another. The space extends into a garden divided into areas planted with grass and a vegetable garden, where the swimming pool is also located. A little further on, toward the east, the vast expanse of the landscape comes into view. As the architect points out: "The idea of a plain is not conveyed by the amount of land, but, indirectly, by the amount of sky." To the west, in fact, "the air outlines the blue profile of the mountain."

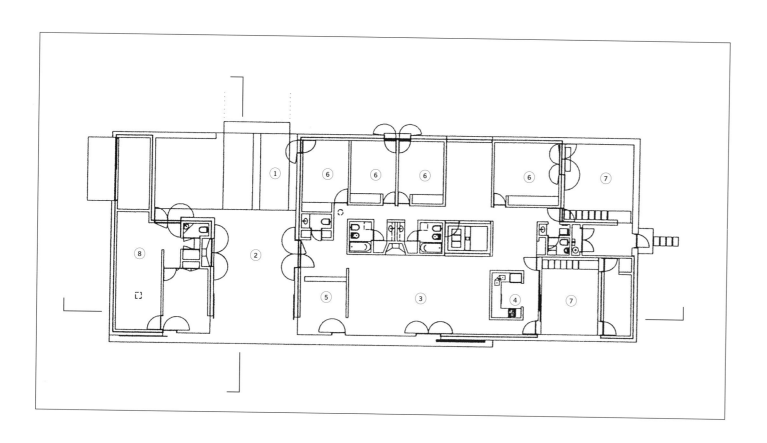

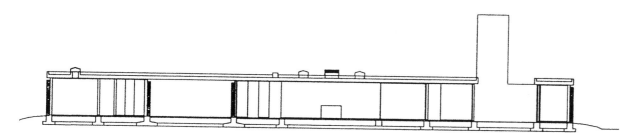

Plan and longitudinal section. Legend 1 garage 2 entrance 3 living room
4 kitchen 5 studio 6 bedrooms 7 patio 8 guests' bedroom.

South, north and west elevations and cross section.

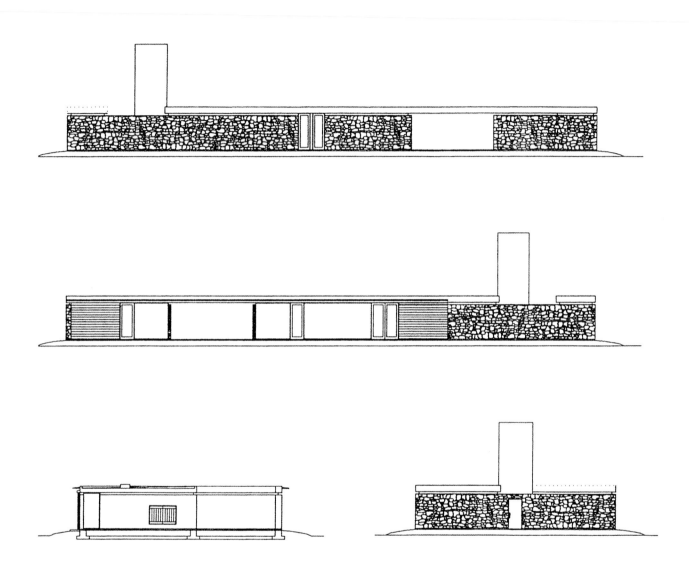

Views of the north front.

Views of the south and north fronts.

View of the north front at night.

Internal views of the living room.

13 lbc arquitectos / alfonso lópez baz and javier calleja

Alfonso López Baz (Mexico City, 1947) and Javier Calleja (Mexico City, 1944) have been practicing the profession together since 1971, the year in which they both graduated from the UNAM in Mexico City. In 1987, they formed the group LBC Arquitectos. They have taught at various universities and exhibited their work abroad as well. Their studio has tackled numerous themes, from housing to offices and from interior design to spaces devoted to culture and recreation, coordinating interdisciplinary groups of specialists (city planning, architecture, design, lighting, acoustics). Their works have been published in the principal international magazines and received a series of awards. Among their recent projects, numerous detached houses (house in the Paseo del Pedregal, 1989; house at Querétaro, 1991; house at Celaya, 1994; house at Monte Líbano, 1995; house at Las Lomas, 1996; house at La Punta, 1997) and, again in Mexico City: the Teatro de las Artes (1994) and the Vertientes (1997); Tabachines (with Moisés Becker, 1998); and Península (1998) residential buildings. Works currently under construction: a house at Monterrey; four houses at Punta Mita, Nayarit; a house on the Costa de Careyes, Jalisco; an estate at Valle de Bravo and a residential district at Cancún.

house at bosques de santa fe mexico city 2003

design
Alfonso López Baz and Javier
Calleja
with Alejandro Sánchez and José
Luis Quiroz
structure
Arturo Hernández
works supervisor
Alejandro González
fixtures
NLZ INSTALA
client
private
location
Bosques de Santa Fe, Mexico City

dimensions
1300 sqm site area
650 sqm built area

dates
2001–02: project
2002–03: construction

The house is located on the grounds of the Golf Club situated on the western fringes of Mexico City, in a gully between two hills where there used to be a bed of sand. For this reason, the architects have had to comply with very strict building regulations, placing precise restrictions on the limits and occupation of the lot, the choice of materials and colors and even the type of plants in the gardens. The house is divided into four blocks that adapt to the steep slope of the ground. At the level of the road are located the car park and the access yard, which leads to a second courtyard, set at a lower level, where a pool of water separates the zone of the services from the large stone volume of the hall, around which the various areas of the house are laid out. A glazed volume with a metal structure on two levels contains, in the upper part, the common zone, made up of lounge, dining room and kitchen, and, in the lower one, the master bedroom and living room. From here stairs lead down to the lowest level, which houses a gym and the children's bedrooms. Only the north-facing fronts are closed because of the wind, while to the east, south and west the various rooms open onto the gardens. The position of the roof of the day zone allows the hours of sunlight to be increased to the maximum in the winter season and permits a view of the mountains surrounding the valley of Mexico. A skylight located between the block of the hall and the common zone illuminates the wardrobe and the main bathroom of the master bedroom. Most of the house's walls are faced with local stone, subjected to a process of oxidation to bring it within the range of colors permitted by the building standards of the district. The most interesting aspect of the project lies in the quest for variety within uniformity, in an attempt to meet the challenge of building a house different from the others—notwithstanding the stringent rules—but which fits perfectly into the context.

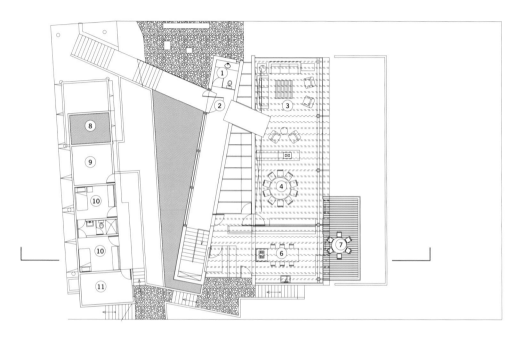

Plans of the access, lower second and lower third floors. Legend 1 bathroom
2 entrance hall 3 living room 4 dining room 5 larder 6 kitchen 7 terrace 8 cistern
9 technical room 10 spare bedroom 11 laundry 12 TV room 13 wardrobe
14 double bedroom 15 bathroom / wardrobe 16 bedroom 17 gym.

Cross section and west elevation.

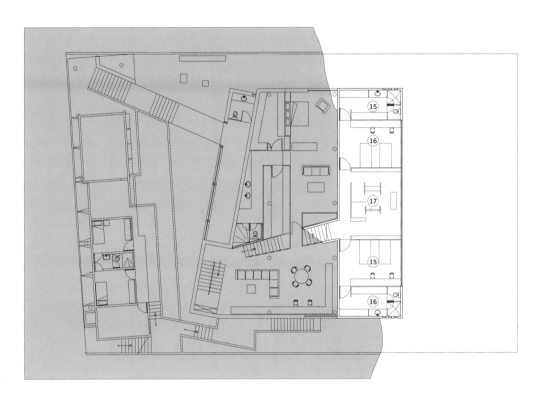

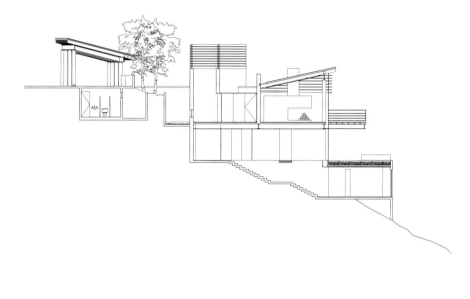

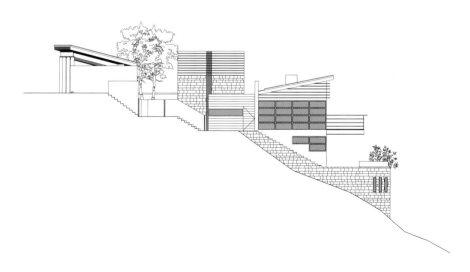

Views from the west and of the front facing the garden.

Details of the entrance area.

Detail of the glass fireplace and internal view of the living room.

14 lcm / fernando romero

Fernando Romero (Mexico City, 1971) graduated in architecture from the Iberoamerican University in 1995. He worked with Rem Koolhaas at the OMA studio in Rotterdam from 1997 to 2000, helping to draw up the project that won the competition for the Casa della Musica in Oporto, Portugal. In 2000 he opened his own studio and in 2005 founded LAR with the aim of seeking new approaches to the practice of architecture through continual spatial and structural experimentation, developing new materials and systems of construction. He has carried out academic activities as a visiting professor at Columbia University in New York (2004) and the School of Architecture of the Javerian University of Colombia in 2005. His work has been included in many exhibitions in Mexico and abroad and he has received numerous awards: GLT 2002-Global Leader of Tomorrow / WEF; FX International Interior Design Awards, 2003; Miami Biennial, 2003; The Architectural League-Young Architects, New York, 2004; Vanceva Design Award, 2004; finalist for the International Bauhaus Award, 2004; SARA-Prize 2005. Among the most significant works realized in Mexico City: Casa M (1998); residences for artists (2000); Banca Inbursa in Paseo de la Reforma (2001); Lomas Studio (2003); House for the Elderly of the Lebanese Club (2003); Palmas office building (2003) and Panorama Tower in Santa Fe (2005). In Japan he has built a public structure in Kanazawa (2004), while in China, his Jin Dong Tea House in Jinhua City (2005) has just been completed. Among the projects under construction: the Museum of Traditional Latin-American and European Art, Palmas II residential and commercial building, office building in Montes Urales, residential district in the historic center and school at Tlalpan, all in the Mexican capital; and then the Auditorio Jalisco, a school and shopping center at Veracruz, the Border Museum at Matamoros, the Immigration Museum-Bridge and the International Holocaust Museum in El Paso, Texas, the Immigration Museum of New Americans in San Diego.

casa ixtapa zihuatanejo guerrero mexico 2001

design
LCM / Fernando Romero
collaborators
Mark Seligson, Juan Pablo Maza,
Carlos Tejeda, Víctor Jaime,
Martín Palardy, Aarón Hernández,
Iván Arellano, Raúl Vivar,
Mauricio Rodriguez Pájaro
structure
DYS Ingeniería SA
consultants
DIIN Instalaciones SA (plant)
Arquitectura Automática (lighting)
INTER Ingeniería y
Construcciones SA (services)
works supervisor
René Cruz
client
private
location
Punta Ixtapa, Zihuatanejo,
Guerrero, Mexico

dimensions
3792 sqm site area
1349 sqm built area

dates
2000: project
2001: construction

The house is situated on a private beach—an exceptional site, in the wonderful climate of the Mexican Pacific coast, where the sun shines almost every day of the year—and accommodates a large family during vacations. With the idea of preserving the traditional style, the local planning regulations require, among other things, construction in stone, the use of natural colors and roofs covered with palm leaves or tiles. In compliance with these regulations, the design combines materials and techniques used in the region—in addition to the *palapa* of the roof, outer walls and floors in plastered and whitewashed reinforced concrete, wooden window frames with a steel structure and facings treated with polymer varnish—and contains the house within a single envelope that, folding back on itself, distinguishes the common spaces from the private ones. The day zone consists of a large living room, surrounded by a solid shell that contains the services (kitchen, hurricane shelter, bathrooms), while the private area is located on the upper floor and is made up of the bedrooms, almost identical but with three different types of bathroom. The curve of the plan models the staircase, which becomes a true channel of internal distribution and comes to an end next to a sinuous light well. The volume of the building seems to have been organically molded by the erosion of the wind and the waves, carving out terraces, empty spaces and passageways. The living room, heart of family life, is conceived as a refuge in the rock, enfolded by a continuous internal space. This room opens up completely to the horizon of the ocean and the garden, where the shape of the swimming pool appears to be trying to tame the surrounding nature.

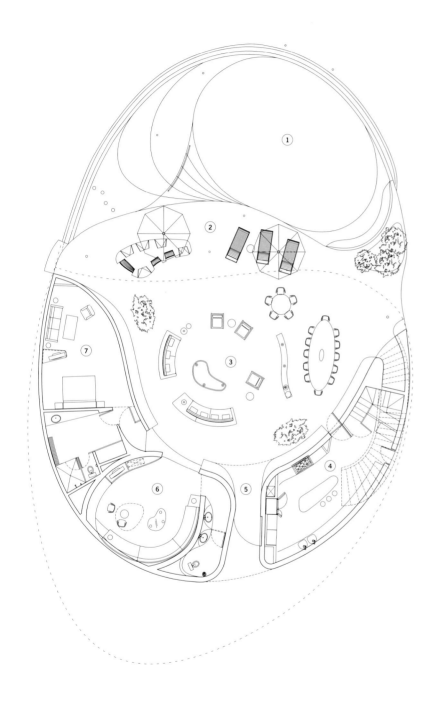

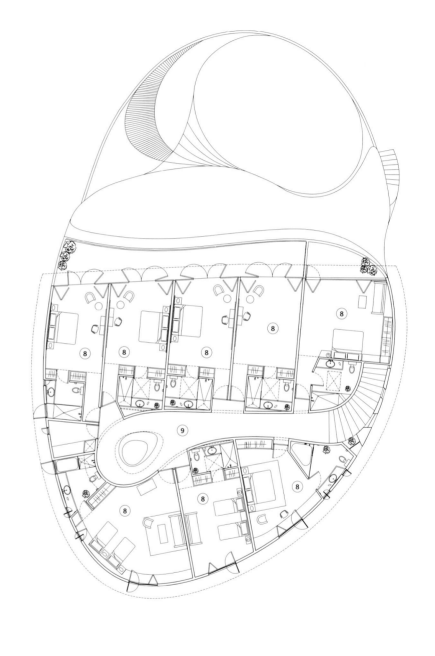

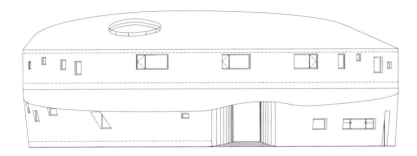

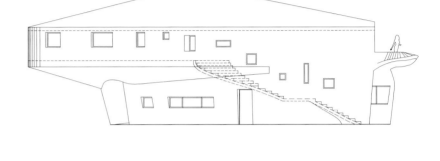

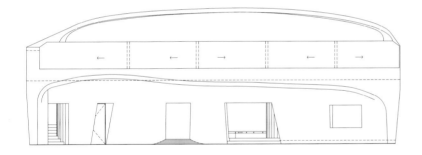

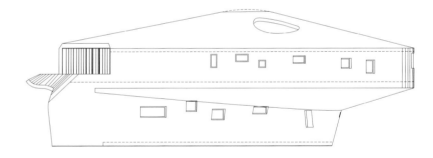

Plans of the ground and second floors. Legend 1 swimming pool 2 terrace
3 living area 4 kitchen 5 entrance 6 TV room 7 master bedroom 8 bedroom
9 corridor.

Elevations.

Views of the entrance front, with the passage right through the house, and of the terrace with the open-air living area.

View of the open-air living area at night and panorama of the bay beyond the swimming pool.

The light well above the hall that provides access to the bedrooms on the second floor.

Views of the staircase from above and below.

15 paulo mendes da rocha

Paulo Archias Mendes da Rocha (Vitória, Espírito Santo, 1928) graduated in 1954 from the Faculty of Architecture of Mackenzie University in São Paulo. At the invitation of João Batista Vilanova Artigas, he has taught since 1962 at the Faculty of Architecture of São Paulo University, where he was made a full professor in 1998. The winner of several competitions, he designed the Brazilian Pavilion for Expo '70 in Osaka, in Japan (1969) and was one of the finalists in the competition for the Georges Pompidou Cultural Center in Paris (1971). In addition to the Serra Dourada stadium at Goiânia (1973), his most important works include, in São Paulo, the Paulistano Athletics Club (1958), Casa PMR (1960), the Guaimbê Building (1964), the chapel of São Pedro at Campos do Jordão (1987–89), Casa Gerassi (1988), the Brazilian Sculpture Museum (1988), the layout of Praça do Patriarca (1992–2002), the Masetti Residence (1995), the FIESP Cultural Center (1996) and the Government Services Center of Itaquera (1998). He has given lectures and held seminars at various Brazilian and foreign institutions. An exhibition of his work was held at the Architectural Association School of Architecture of London in 1999 and he was selected as representative of Brazilian architecture for the Venice Biennale of Architecture in 2000. Since 1985 he has worked in partnership with Argenton Colonelli and Weliton Ricoy Torres, with whom he drew up the master plan for the restoration and extension of the Faculty of Medicine and designed the Administrative Center of Ciba Geigy-Novartis, the renovation of the José Inocéncio da Costa School, the IV Centenario housing complex and the seat of the Public Ministry of São Paulo state. He won the Mies van der Rohe Prize for Latin America with his restoration of the Pinacoteca do Estado in São Paulo (1998). The importance of his work was recognized with the award of the Pritzker Prize in 2006.

casa prata arcuschin são paulo brazil 2005

design
Paulo Mendes da Rocha
collaborators
Meter Arquitetos
Martin Corullon, Joana Elito,
Anna Ferrari, Gustavo Cedroni
structure
Zaven Kurkdjian
works supervisor
Ary Breinis
fixtures
MA2 Engenharia
client
Isabella Prata and Idel Arcuschin
location
Rua Carlos Millan, São Paulo,
Brazil

dimensions
930 sqm site area
590 sqm built area

dates
2001: project
2003–05: construction

"[...] It is the design of a Brazilian garden. The trees are all fruit trees and the ground is of packed earth, clean. There is a water tank and a pit for dead leaves and rotten fruit. To make compost. The fruit is there to be eaten and to attract birds. The house will have two living rooms: one in the shade and the other in the sun." This simple description accompanies the sketches of the house, underlining the approach that Paulo Mendes da Rocha has taken to this new project. The house is composed of a main volume, on two stories, a large terrace and a garden of fruit trees. Both the building and the terrace are raised above street level, leaving a large area free on the ground floor: this is a common feature of his strategy of composition, which has taken the lesson of Le Corbusier on board. Underneath the house, there is nothing but the access to the stairs and a service element for parties. Under the terrace, there is a space for parking cars; the rest of the lot, left unpaved, is a large garden. On the second floor are located the services of the house and the living room, which is connected by a small bridge to the unroofed terrace. This area, on the same level as the living room, is conceived as a raised garden set amongst the crowns of the trees and constitutes its extension into the open air. From the large terrace it is possible to go back down to ground level by an alternative route consisting of a metal bridge and a staircase set against the side wall. The third floor is occupied by three bedrooms, each with its own bathroom. The whole construction is in whitewashed reinforced concrete and the structure of the main volume, measuring 21 × 12 meters, consists of two main longitudinal beams, each resting on three pillars. The terrace, which measures 6 × 30 meters, is supported at each end and on a pair of central pillars. The layout of the house, with its setbacks from the road and the boundary with the neighbors, is dictated by a rigorous compliance with the local planning regulations.

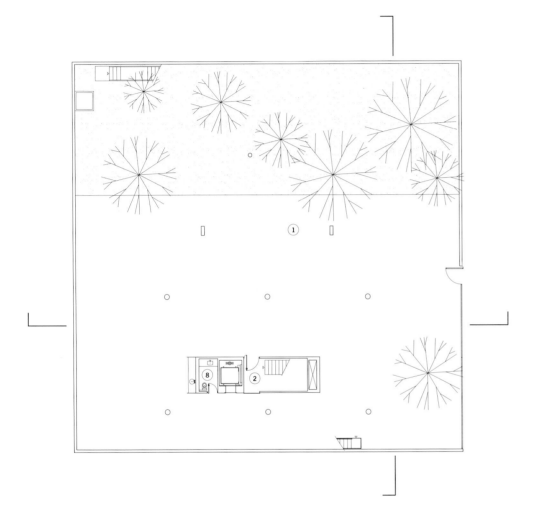

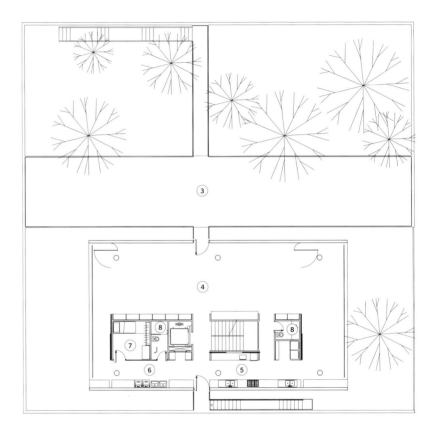

Plans of the ground, second and third floor. Legend 1 garage 2 entrance hall 3 veranda 4 living room 5 kitchen 6 laundry 7 spare bedroom 8 bathroom 9 corridor 10 bedroom 11 wardrobe.

Sections.

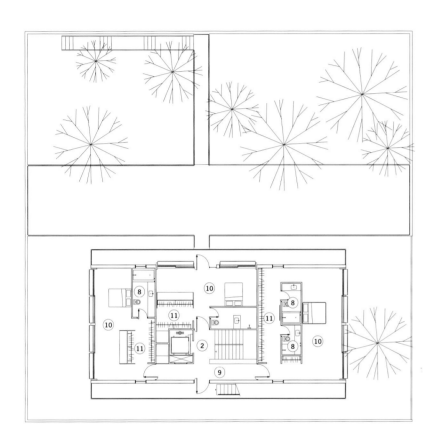

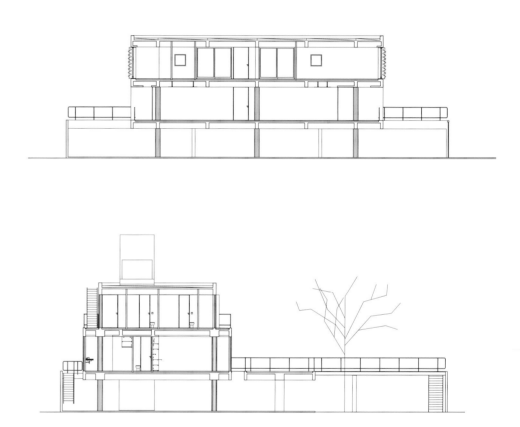

Details of the parking area and the entrance under the porches.

View from the north.

View of the south front from the front terrace.

Views of the terrace from opposite ends.

Internal views of the kitchen and dining area.

Views of the day zone.

16 mmbb arquitetos / angelo bucci

Angelo Bucci (Orlândia, São Paulo, 1963) graduated from the Faculty of Architecture and City Planning of São Paulo University (FAUUSP) in 1987, where he also took a master's degree (1998) and a doctorate (2005). He has collaborated with Aflalo & Gasperini Arquitetos (1987–88), Marcelo Fragelli (1988–89), Eduardo de Almeida (1994–95) and Paulo Mendes da Rocha (1996–2002). From 1996 to 2002, he was a member of the MMBB studio, based in São Paulo, along with the architects Fernando de Mello Franco, Marta Moreira and Milton Braga. In 2003 he founded SPBR Arquitetos. Since 2001 he has been teaching at the FAUUSP and, in 2005, was visiting professor at Arizona State University in Phoenix, and at Andrés Bello University in Santiago, Chile. Among the many recognitions he has received, including the Jóvenes Arquitetos per la Posada Prize at Juquehy, São Sebastião (1993–98), he was a finalist for the Mies van der Rohe prize for Latin America in 2001 and received an award for the Trianon Underground Parking Lot project at the 4th São Paulo International Biennial of Architecture in 1999 and for a residence a Riberão Preto in 2003, while in 2002 he won the competition for the Memorial of the Republic at Piracicaba. Among his constructed works, several detached houses: house at Orlândia, 1992–94; house at Perdizes, 1996–98; house at Carapicuiba, 2003; house at Santa Teresa, Rio de Janeiro, 2004; the offices of an advertising agency in São Paulo (1994); a dentistry clinic at Orlândia (2000); and Casa Mello at Riberão Preto (2000–01).

detached house aldeia da serra brazil 2002

design
MMBB Arquitetos
Angelo Bucci, Milton Braga,
Fernando de Mello Franco,
Marta Moreira
collaborators
André Drummond, Eduardo
Ferroni, Maria Julia Herklotz,
Anna Helena Vilella
structure
Ibsen Pulleo Uvo
building contractors
Paulo Balugoli, Nelson Cabeli
clients
José Henrique and Beatriz Arruda
Mariante
location
Aldeia da Serra, Brazil

dimensions
800 sqm site area
256 sqm built area

dates
2001: design
2002: construction

Situated in the suburbs of São Paulo, the house has a highly expressive structure of reinforced concrete. The superimposition of two cellular floor slabs defines a box of cement and glass inserted in a lot measuring 20 × 40 meters that has a marked difference in level between the front and back. The two slabs (16.20 meters on a side, with cells of 90 × 90 centimeters), are suspended above the ground by four pillars with square sections. The rigorously geometric character of the plan is attenuated by a number of compositional stratagems that identify uses and views: in fact the asymmetry permits a suitable functional organization, while an empty space, located slightly off center, contains the two flights of stairs, extending for three levels, and illuminates the utility rooms. Large sliding glass doors characterize the front and rear: the entrance is set in the main front, counterbalanced, on the right, by the volume of the water tank, supported by one of the columns; on the front facing onto the garden are juxtaposed two walkways suspended at different heights, connecting the rooms inside to the surrounding terrain. The treatment of the lateral façades is more uniform, although still differentiated by the refined effect of suspension on the west side, where the night zone is located, from the east side, where the heavier volume of the living room fireplace emerges. The roof, covered with a pool of water, can be traversed on a pathway made of slabs of concrete.

Plans of the ground and second floors. Legend 1 Parking area 2 access staircase 3 spare bedroom 4 studio and workshop 5 bathroom 6 entrance 7 living room 8 terrace 9 kitchen 10 study 11 bedroom 12 double bedroom.

North, south and west elevations and sections.

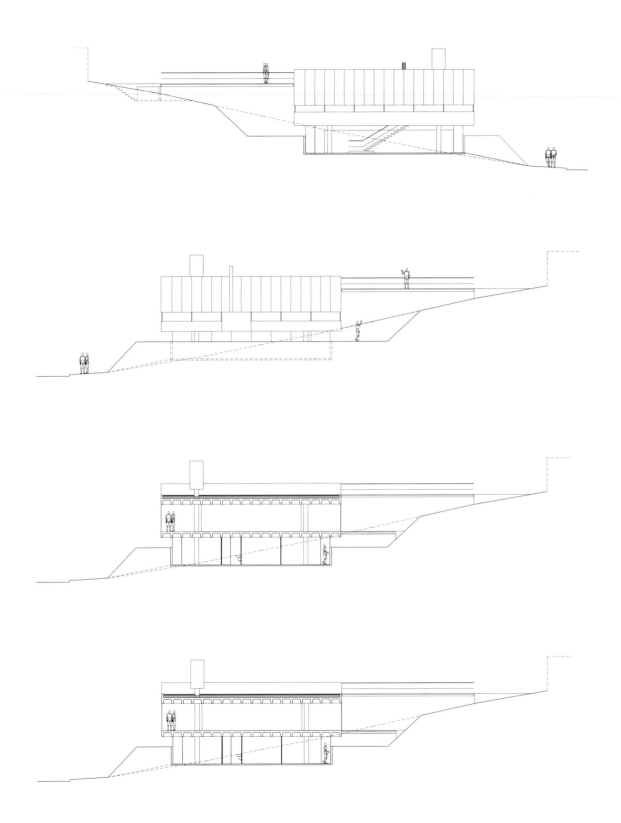
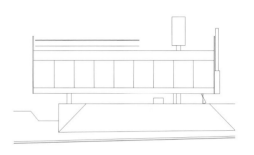
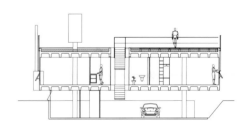

View of the main front with the water tank raised above the roof.

View of the south front of the living room.

Views of the east front with the gangway connecting roof and garden.

Details of the staircase leading to the roof and the projection toward the road.

View of the living room from the terrace at the rear in the evening and internal view of the dining room.

View of the east front at night.

17

procter & rihl

Christopher Procter (Philadelphia, 1956), graduated from Carnegie-Mellon University (USA) in 1979, and from the Architectural Association of London in 1987. He has also carried out studies in Japan and with Paolo Solari at Arcosanti (Arizona, 1978). He has collaborated with several professional studios in the United States (Rick Mather Architects, Allies and Morrison, Sheppard Robson) and the United Kingdom (Jestico + Whiles), taking an interest in the question of solar energy as well. Fernando Rihl (Porto Alegre, 1962) graduated from the Architectural Association of London in 1998, after taking a diploma at the Federal University of Rio Grande do Sul (UFRGS) in Brazil, in 1989, where he also taught for two years. Named the best student of architecture in Brazil in 1989, he has been a senior lecturer at the Chelsea College of Art and Design and visiting tutor at Oxford Brookes. Members of the Royal Institute of British Architects, Procter & Rihl have received various prizes—Visual Arts Awards, London, 1998; 4th Biennial of Latin-American Architecture, 2004; RIBA Award 2005 for Casa Slice—and have taken part in international exhibitions in France, Portugal, Peru, Japan, Italy, the United States and Australia. They have been practicing together since 1995. Among their recent projects, numerous renovations in London; two detached houses in Vermont, and Poa, Brazil (both in 2004); the extension of the Totteridge Conservatory, Great Britain (2003); the renovation of the Robert Bowman Gallery of London (2003); and Office Lofts on Grimsby Street, Shoreditch, Great Britain (2002).

casa slice porto alegre brazil 2004

design
Christopher Procter, Fernando Rihl
collaborators
Dirk Anderson, James Backwell,
Johannes Lobbert
structure
Michael Baigent MBOK
Antonio Pasquali
Vitor Pasin
building contractors
JS Construções
works supervisor
Mauro Medeiros
fixtures
Flavio Mainardi
client
Neusa Oliveira
location
Avenida Bastian and
Rua Baroneza do Gravatão,
Porto Alegre, RS, Brazil

dimensions
164 sqm site area
200 sqm built area

dates
2002: project
2004: construction

Interested in the potentialities of residual areas in the urban context that have been left unutilized, Procter & Rihl took on the challenge of a difficult, extremely long and narrow lot, with the idea of exploring the design possibilities offered by the site. Starting out from an existing house, the renovation proposes a complex geometry that generates a series of illusory spatial effects inside the building. The new house meets the requirements of the functional program by making the most of natural light, keeping the need to resort to air conditioning to a minimum through control of solar radiation and ventilation. The design makes references to modern Brazilian architecture—in the sculptural definition of the volumes in concrete, adopting local building techniques, although the finishings are more restrained and precise; in the large spaces opening onto the outside, with the vegetation used as a genuine tool of composition—without renouncing the use of several elements of British origin: the attention to detail, the use of prefabricated components, the naturalistic and informal bedding of the equatorial plants, more common in the tradition of the English garden. The brut style, typical of Brazilian modernism, is evident in the use of concrete cast in wooden formwork, while British precision is revealed in the construction with modular steel components and the handling of the details of the metal facing of the front, roof, gutters and reticular sun blinds of the windows. Instead of seeking to neutralize the length of the site, Procter & Rihl decided to turn this constraint to positive use. A series of deviations from orthogonality models the space, which expands and contracts inside a prism, distorting its perception: the walls and inclined ceilings dilate the rooms in a virtual manner, as the observer's gaze is guided toward more distant planes, with an effect of continual expansion. In this way, the internal space is enriched with situations that are always changing as the observer's point of view shifts. The location of the entrance on the narrowest end, the height of the day zone and the design of the stairs and courtyard help to confer an unexpected depth on the domestic environment. The experimentation has also extended to the care taken over the details through the use of craft techniques, as well as the recycling of materials found during construction and the design of some pieces of furniture. The swimming pool, suspended above the living room, is conceived as a dynamic element that produces different light effects over the course of the day and night.

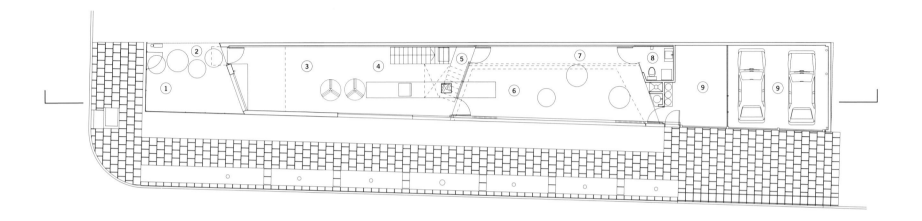

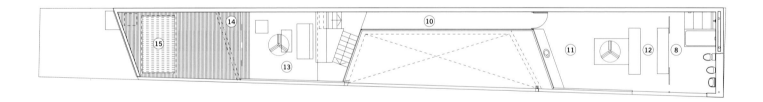

Plan of the ground and second floors. Legend 1 garden 2 entrance
3 living room 4 dining room 5 kitchen 6 inner courtyard 7 corridor 8 bathroom
9 garage 10 hall 11 bedroom 12 wardrobe 13 guests' bedroom 14 terrace
15 swimming pool.

West elevation and longitudinal section.

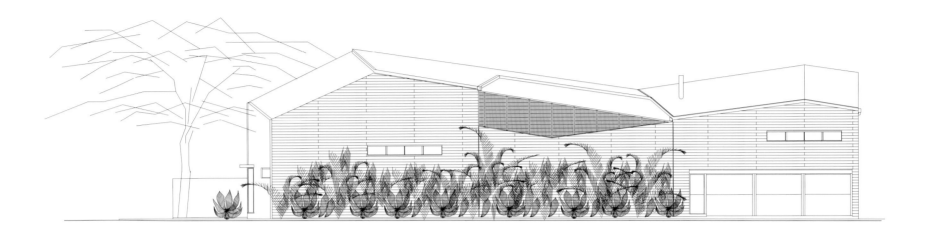

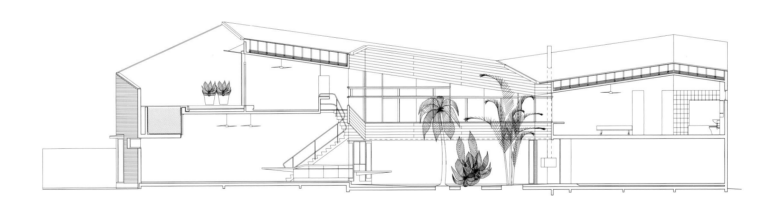

Aerial view.

The south front and view from the street at night.

The inner courtyard.

Views of the dining and living rooms.

196

Detail of the stairs and view of the guests' bedroom.

18 smiljan radic

Smiljan Radic Clarke (Santiago, Chile, 1965) graduated in architecture from the Pontifical Catholic University of Chile in 1989 and then went on to study at the School of Architecture in Venice (IUAV). In 1993 he won, together with the architects Nikolas Skutelis and Flavio Zanon, the competition for the design of Plateia Eleftheria ("Liberty Square") in Iraklion, Greece. Returning to Chile, in 1994 he won, with Teodoro Fernández Larrañaga and Cecilia Puga Larraín, the competition for the Sergio Larraín Garcia-Moreno Latin-American Information and Documentation Center in Santiago (1994–96). In 2001 he was named the best Chilean architect under the age of thirty-five. Professor of architectural design at the School of Architecture of the Pontifical Catholic University of Chile, he practices in partnership with the sculptress Marcela Correa. His principal projects include: a pier on Lake Rapel (1990); a sculpture workshop in Santiago (1994); Casa Chica at Talca (1995–96); an office building at Chonchi, Chiloé (1995–96); Casa Fundo Los Maitenes at Melipilla (with Ricardo Serpell) and Casa San Clemente at Talca; the Sustainable Development Center at Coinguillo-Temuco (1997); the square in the municipality of San Pedro in Melipilla; the restoration of a church at Chiloé; the Agua restaurant in Santiago and the R3 prototype (a one-roomed apartment), realized with Gonzalo Puga). Together with Eduardo Castillo and Ricardo Serpell, he won the competition for the design of the civic quarter and public buildings at Concepción in 2000 (currently under construction). In addition to the house at Nercón (1999, winner of the ProCobre Prize for the best architectural design at the 12th Chilean Biennial of Architecture), his most recent works include: the house for his sister (2002), Casa Carpentier and Casa CR, all three in Santiago (2003); Casa K6 at Marbella and the copper house at Talca (2004); a detached house at Rancagua (2005–06).

casa pite at papudo chile 2005

design
Smiljan Radic Clarke
collaborators
Loreto Lyon, Danilo Lazcano
Gonzalo Torres (model)
Hugo Lagos (photographs
of model)
structure
Ingenieros Valladares
works supervisor
Manual Arriagada
building contractors
Constructora Los Alerces
consultants
Interdesign, Eduardo Godoy
(lighting)
Héctor Acuña (electrics)
Jorge Jaña (heating)
Enrique Manrique (plant)
client
María Teresa Petric,
Rodrigo Peón Veiga
location
Papudo, Quinta Región, Chile

dimensions
15,000 sqm site area
400 sqm built area
795 sqm external area

dates
2003: project
2003–05: construction

Located in the midst of the inhospitable nature of the central coast of Chile, Casa Pite has been built on very large plot of land. The various sections of the house are distributed over the entire surface of the site, giving the intervention an exceptional character. A coastal road runs along the highest part of the plot, about forty meters above sea level; from it a driveway leads down the slope covered with native scrub. Further down, an area parallel to the sea underlines the contrast between the gentle upper slope and the crevices filled with cactus below. At this level is set the access platform, a ramp that runs down to the terrace on which the swimming pool and the main rooms of the complex are located: the lounge, kitchen, master bedroom, bathrooms and cellar. Walking past these, along an external passageway that skirts the edge of the cliff, you come to the bedrooms for guests. The third level—eighteen meters lower down—is located at the border between the crevices and the veined granite rocks of the seafront. This where the space of the villa for the children is set. The various sectors are linked by outdoor ramps raised above the wild vegetation. Each of them establishes, on the base of its form and position, a specific relationship with the seascape: the central pavilion is raised above the ocean as if stood on piles; the guests' bedrooms conjure up the image of a cave to foster the sensation of a certain distance; the children's ones have been constructed practically "in the sea," as close as possible to the line on which the waves break on stormy days. From the outset, the client insisted on the fact that the villa should be completely invisible from the road. Thanks to the collaboration of the sculptress Marcela Correa, eleven blocks of basalt from a quarry 450 kilometers away have been placed on the access platform, with the aim of burying the house under the weight of their material.

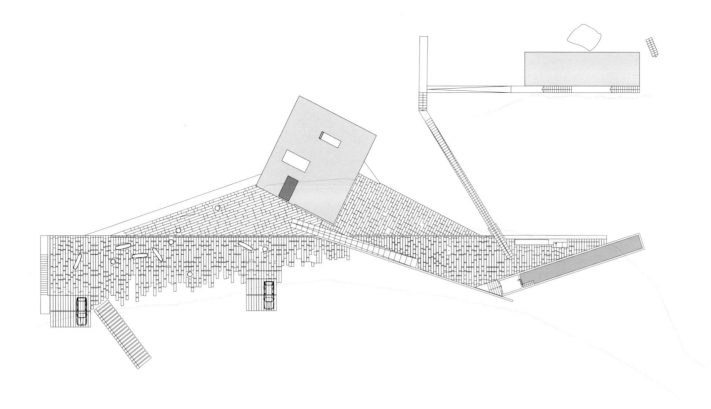

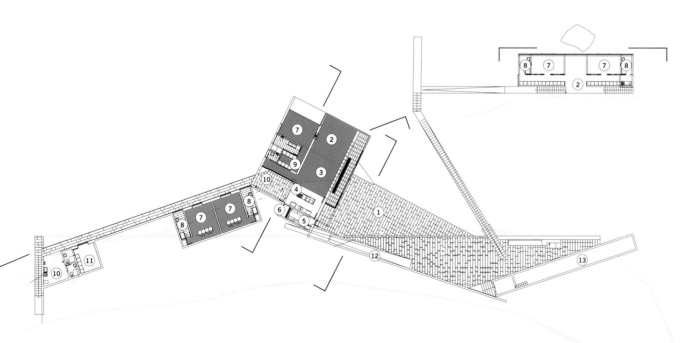

Plan of the terrace.
Plan of the ground floors. Legend 1 terrace 2 living room 3 dining room
4 kitchen 5 larder 6 cellar 7 bedroom 8 bathroom 9 wardrobe
10 courtyard 11 spare bedroom 12 ramp 13 swimming pool.

Sections.

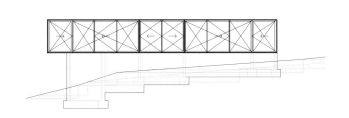

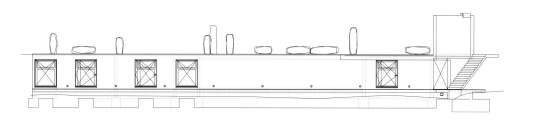

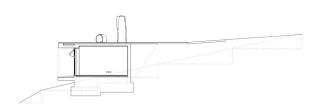

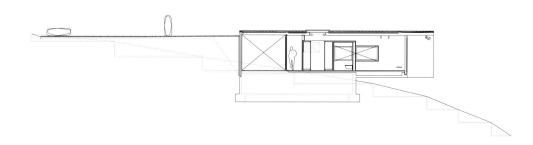

Views from the sea and of the roof terrace.

Views of the block housing the children's bedrooms from above and of the over hanging living room from below.

The block of the children's bedrooms near the shore.

The running balcony leading to the guests' bedrooms.

The entrance route leading up the slope.

View of the terrace in front of the living and dining rooms at night.

Detail of a sliding glass door.

The staircase at the end of the house that links the upper parking area to the entrance route overlooking the sea.

Panoramic view with one of the blocks of basalt in the foreground.

External view of the main block and view of the access terrace.

19

michel rojkind

Michel Rojkind (Mexico City, 1969) graduated from the Iberoamerican University in 1994. From 1993 to 1998, he practiced the profession independently. From 1999 to 2002, he went into partnership with Isaac Broid and Miquel Adriá, with whom he realized around twenty works. In 2000–01 he was curator of the FWD section, specializing in technology, of the well-known Mexican magazine *Arquine*. In 2002 he embarked on a new phase in his career and founded Rojkind Arquitectos. In 2004, together with Tatiana Bilbao, Arturo Ortiz and Derek Dellekamp, he set up the MXDF Center of Multidisciplinary Urban Research, whose objective is to intervene in specific areas of Mexican urban development through systematic studies of the social, political, cultural and environmental conditions of the territory, in collaboration with various national and international academic institutions (National Autonomous University of Mexico; Iberoamerican University; Anahuac University; La Salle University of Mexico City; Studio Basel, ETH, Switzerland; Architectural Association of London; MIT, Boston, Massachusetts). In 2005 he was included by *Architectural Record* in the list of the ten best "avant-garde designers." He has been a visiting professor at the Autonomous University of Mexico (2001–02), the Anahuac University Campus Norte (2003–04) and the Iberoamerican University (2005). Among the main works constructed in Mexico City, it is worth mentioning: the Tlaxcala 190 residential building and the Videoteca Nacional Educativa (2002); the MP3 Building at Colonia Condesa (2003) and Falcón Building at San Angel (2004). Currently under construction: a hotel at Oaxaca; the City Santa Fe commercial and residential building; the master plans for Lincoln Park, Masarik (square and underground parking) and Irapuato (cultural expo); a building in Miami (with Derek Dellekamp); the Morelia Michoacán center of biomedical research and a residential building at Bosque de Canelos, Mexico City.w

casa pr 34 tecamachalco mexico 2004

design
Michel Rojkind
collaborators
Agustín Pereyra, Beatriz Díaz,
Alvaro Sordo, María Carrillo,
Gianpaolo Fussari
structure
Jorge Cadena
works supervisor
Factor Eficiencia
Fermín Espinosa
Ricardo Brito
consultants
José Ignacio Báez, Jesús Saldaña
(fixtures)
Luciano Alvarez (carpentry)
Esrawe Diseño, Mob, Jorge
Mdahuar, Acrílico Ramón Flores
(interiors)
Dupont (painting)
Ambiente Fritz Sigg (landscaping)
client
private
location
Tecamachalco

dimensions
960 sqm site area
136 sqm built area

dates
2002: project
2004: construction

The design challenge commenced with the renovation of a house dating from the late sixties, located at Tecamachalco, in Mexico State. The intervention made the spaces more transparent and the distribution of functions more efficient. The decision to build a further extension on the roof, with the construction of an independent house, has led to the creation of two separate accesses, with the introduction of a spiral staircase leading to the new structure. The domestic space is divided into two blocks staggered by half a story (public and private): the first, corresponding to the access level, contains the living room, dining room, kitchen, bathroom and a hoist that rises from the entrance; half a story lower are set the TV room and master bedroom, with bathroom and wardrobe. Without neglecting the contribution of the extraordinary Mexican workers, innovative materials and bright colors have been utilized: the structure is built out of steel sections; the roof has been carefully covered with sheets of metal, as if it were a ship or a space shuttle (there are two panels of mineral wool under this membrane to provide insulation and soundproofing); the inside, finally, is lined with chipboard made from large chips, finished with white resin. The roof on which this new volume stands becomes a large terrace, where the existing skylights of the original house have been transformed into translucent acrylic seats. Evoking the image of a dance between two moving bodies, the sensual form of the architecture, with an envelope that changes direction at every curve, was inspired by the ballerina who was to live in the apartment.

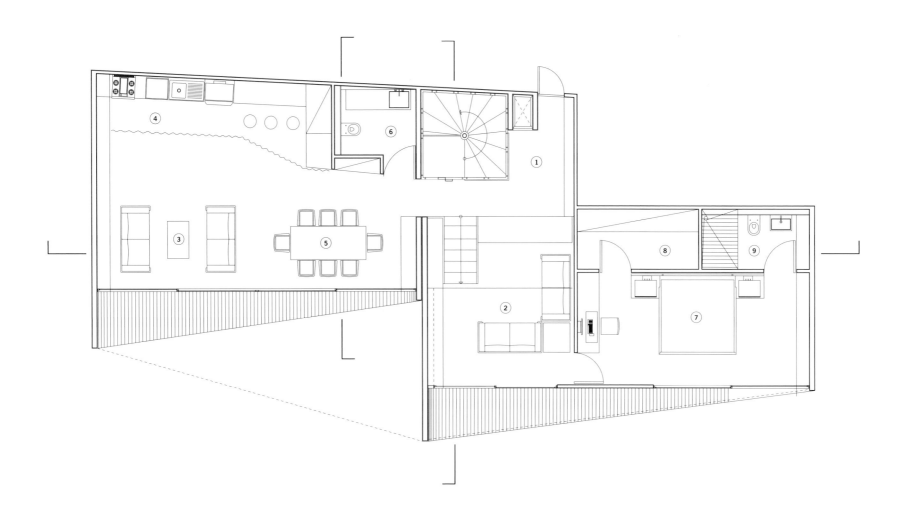

Plan and south elevation. Legend 1 entrance 2 TV room 3 living room 4 kitchen
5 dining room 6 spare bathroom 7 double bedroom 8 wardrobe 9 main bathroom.

Longitudinal section and cross sections of the day zone, wardrobe
of the double bedroom and entrance hall.

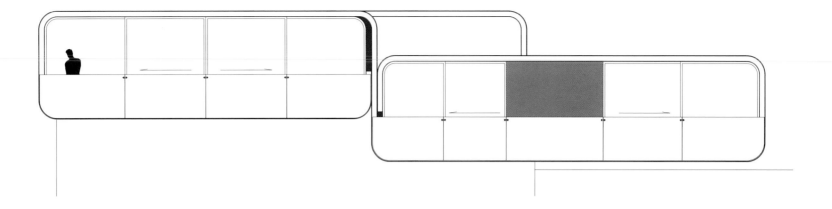

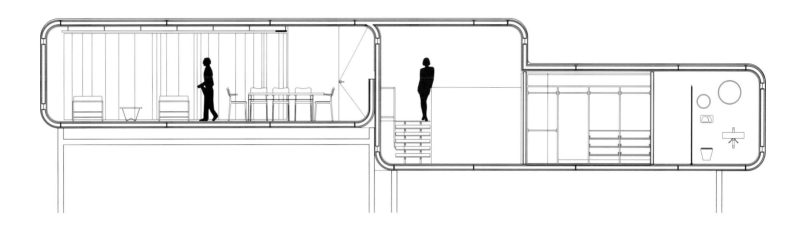

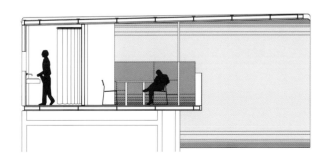

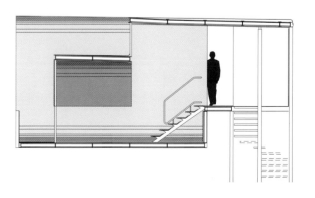

Views of the house in its urban setting and of the roof terrace from the side.

221

Details of the skylights on the roof terrace, transformed into seats made of translucent acrylic.

The balcony of the double bedroom on the south front.

Internal views of the entrance hall and corridor, of the landing of the spiral
staircase from the apartment underneath and of the dining area.

20 cristián undurraga

Cristián Undurraga (Santiago, Chile, 1954) graduated in architecture in 1977, from the Faculty of Architecture of the Pontifical Catholic University, where he has taught since 1999. The same year he was awarded the "Arquitectura Joven" prize at the first Santiago Biennial of Architecture. In 1978 he opened his own professional studio with Ana Luisa Devés, working contemporaneously on themes of design, architecture and city planning. They have taken part in numerous national and international competitions. In 1991 they won the Andrea Palladio International Architecture Prize with the Casa del Cerro. Their work has been exhibited in several countries in the Americas and Europe. Among their most significant projects, we can mention: the renovation of the Barrio Cívico in Santiago (1995); the DUOC UC Foundation (1995–97); the Museum of Modern Art in Valdivia (1998); the Ministry of Public Works in Antofagasta (1998). The most recent works constructed in Santiago include: the Ermita de San Antonio residential district (1996–2000); the Museum of Visual Arts (2000); Casa El Mirador (2001–02), which won a prize at the Quito Biennial of Architecture; the Las Condes City Hall (2002–03) and the Simonetti office building (2004–05). Under construction, the extension of the Palacio de La Moneda in the capital, the seat of the Chilean government, with a cultural center.

house on lake colico chile 2004

design
Cristián Undurraga
Undurraga & Devés Arquitectos
collaborator
Mario Marchant
structure
Jorge Marambio
fixtures
Jorge Herreros
works supervisor
Edgar Schmidt, Rafael Herreros
client
private
location
Lake Colico, Temuco, IX Región
de la Araucanía, Chile

dimensions
5000 sqm site area
400 sqm built area

dates
2003: project
2004: construction

The project tackles the theme of the settlement of a territory—that of Lake Colico in the south of Chile, among the majestic mountains of the Andean Cordillera—in which the landscape has an extraordinary force. Into this essentially geographical scenario is inserted a clear and peremptory volume, located on the southern side, at a height intermediate between the access road and the level of the water. A steep path turns into a winding promenade that runs down to the entrance. The route is cunningly laid out so as to offer panoramic views of the surroundings, until it arrives, crossing a footbridge, at a solid wall of rough concrete and stones. This block is a core of services in which the kitchen, bathrooms, cellar and vertical circulation are arranged in a line. Crossing the threshold, a terrace-belvedere permits contemplation of the unspoiled nature, anticipating the abundant views from inside the building. Through the lightness and transparence of a glass and steel structure extending for three levels, the house seeks to blend into the surrounding wood. The idea is to inhabit every corner of the house, remaining in close contact with the outside. Consequently the free and continuous plan includes three courtyards, which bring the vegetation into the domestic space. Hence these voids are the elements that establish the relationship with nature and separate the various sectors of the day zone (lounge, dining room, studio) from the night zone; but there are also light wells that divide up the space vertically. Conceived in this way, the design, characterized by a rigorous economy of form, utilizes abstraction as a counterpoint to the context. The tension between opposites is evident in the architectural solution: the thick and solid wall—whose tectonics are intended to recall the essential values of the land, even evoking the long-ago history of these places—supports and contrasts with the limpid pavilion, whose immateriality alludes, instead, to modernity.

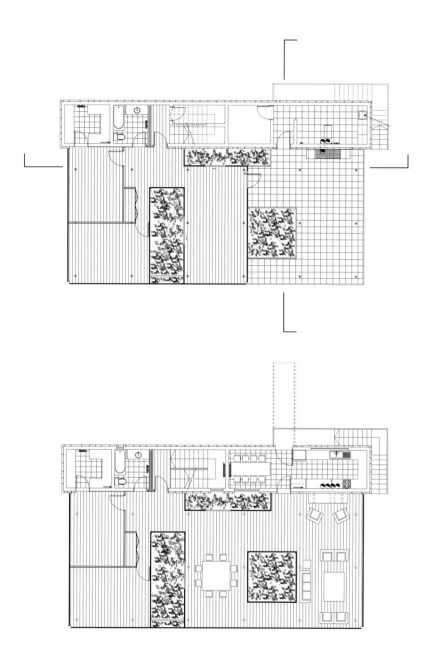
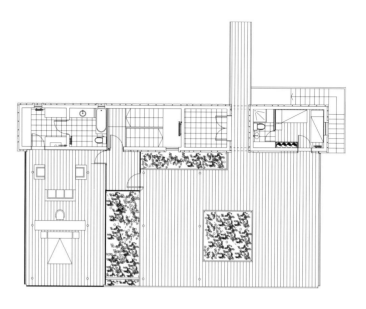

Plans of the ground floor, the second floor and the third floor
with the entrance walkway.

Cross section, east elevation, longitudinal section and west elevation.

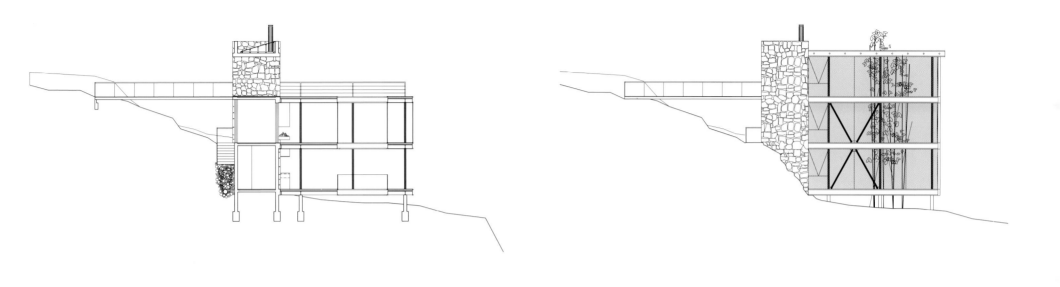

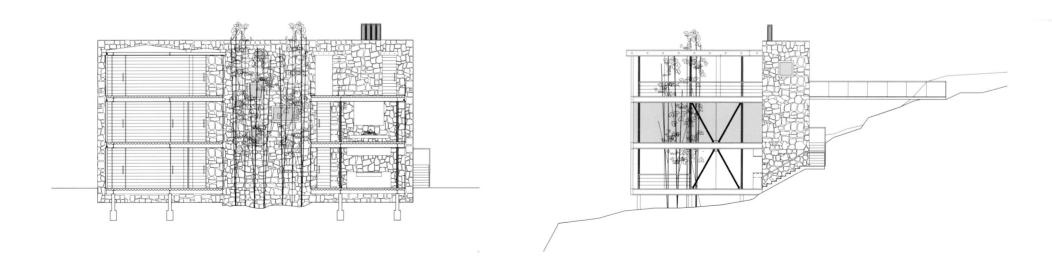

229

The house against the backdrop of the lake and view of the terrace on the upper level.

Views from the northeast and southeast and of the west front.

Details of the day areas on the second floor interspersed and divided up by courtyard-skylight wells with plants.

The panoramic terrace on the roof and details
of the north front and the entrance hall.

contents